GREETING CARDS

A Collection from Around the World

Edited by Takenobu Igarashi

GREETING CARDS

世界のグリーティング・カード

編集＝五十嵐威暢

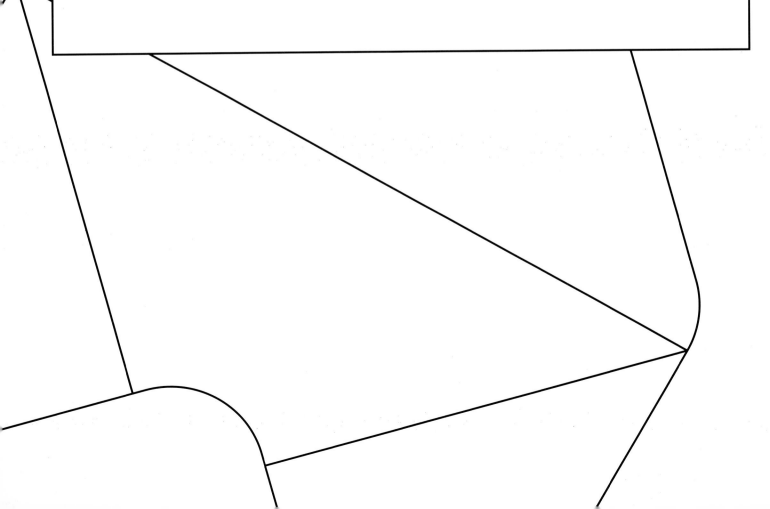

Abbreviations
AD = Art Director
D = Designer
A = Artist
C = Client

GREETING CARDS
A Collection from Around the World

Edited by Takenobu Igarashi © 1989
Published by Graphic-sha Publishing Company Ltd. © 1989

ISBN 4-7661-0537-0

Printed in Japan by Toppan Printing Company Ltd.

First Edition September 1989

Editing and book conception . . . . Takenobu Igarashi
Art direction . . . . Takenobu Igarashi
Cover design . . . . Ross McBride
Layout . . . . Ross McBride
Photography . . . . Ed Ikuta; T. Nacása & Partners
Translations . . . . Scott Brause
English typesetting . . . . Lynx Inc.
Japanese typesetting . . . . Sanwa Typesetting Co., Ltd.
Printing and binding . . . . Toppan Printing Co., Ltd.
Coordinating . . . . Seiki Okuda

Preface
はじめに

Unlike a letter, a greeting card requires a special idea. A pleasing illustration or trick of some kind should support the sort of message it contains, so as to give the receiver the fullest sense of satisfaction. In an effort to do this, designers are forever searching for new ideas, materials and techniques; continually discovering just what is possible within the rigid confines of cost and postal restrictions.

I think there is something human and enjoyable about cutting the envelope, taking the card in hand and opening it, then looking it over and reading it. The message and design meet and play out their story before our very eyes. As you can see from the many fine works presented here, this is a world of design that is full of possibilities.

The fact that no collection of innovative greeting cards had ever been assembled prompted us to publish this book.

Takenobu Igarashi

手紙と違ってグリーティング・カードには,何か特別のアイデアが必要だ。短いコメントを助ける楽しいイラストや意外な仕掛けが,受け取る人に十分な満足感を与えることが肝要である。郵送という手段の制約の中で,デザイナーは日頃からこの分野に情熱を注いできた。

なかでも立体的な構造のものは楽しい。封を切る,手にとる,開ける,見る,読むという手の中の行為。そこで繰り広げられるメッセージとデザインのドラマは,とてもヒューマンで好ましいと思う。

そして本書に収録されている数々の秀作で知ることが出来るように,そのデザインの世界は広く,可能性に満ちている。

しかし,グラフィックデザインの分野でこれほどイノベイティブなグリーティング・カードに関する出版物が見当たらない。このことが本書の出版の動機である。

五十嵐威暢

Paper Show Invitation
USA 1986
LaPine/O'Very
AD, D, A · Traci O'Very Covey
C · Unisource
(Card is pulled from the
envelope by a beer tab)
ペーパー・ショード招待状
（カードはリングを引いて封筒から取り出す）

comes to a head
...es from the most
...flowing with wis-
...e kind that elicit
...mous names as:
...son, **Strathmore,**
...**Mausau, Weyer-**
...**Boise-Cascade,**
...brate their arrival
... and a free bar
...icating brews will
... Main Gallery of
...) from 3 to 8 p.m.
...ents. Cheers.

Christmas Card
Design consultants
England 1987
CarterWong
AD · Phil Carter, Phil Wong
D · Phil Carter, Alison Tomlin
A · Mary Roberts
C · CarterWong
クリスマスカード
デザイン・コンサルティング会社

Season's Greetings Card
Graphic design firm
USA 1983
Crosby Associates Inc.
AD, D · Bart Crosby
C · Crosby Associates Inc.
季節の挨拶状
グラフィックデザイン会社

New Year's Card
Graphic design firm
USA 1985
Crosby Associates Inc.
AD · Bart Crosby
D · Jan Gulley
C · Crosby Associates Inc.
年賀状
グラフィックデザイン会社

'88 New Year's Card
Graphic design firm
USA 1987
Crosby Associates Inc.
AD · Bart Crosby
D · Tim Hartford
C · Crosby Associates Inc.
年賀状
グラフィックデザイン会社

Christmas Card
USA 1987
LaPine/O'Very
AD, D · Julia LaPine
C · Novell, Inc.
クリスマスカード

A pale dove
brings berries
red and green
softly
in his mouth.
May these holidays
bring you
peace enduring.

NOVELL

New Year's Card
USA 1988
M Plus M, Inc.
AD, D, A · Takaaki Matsumoto
C · M Plus M, Inc.
年賀状

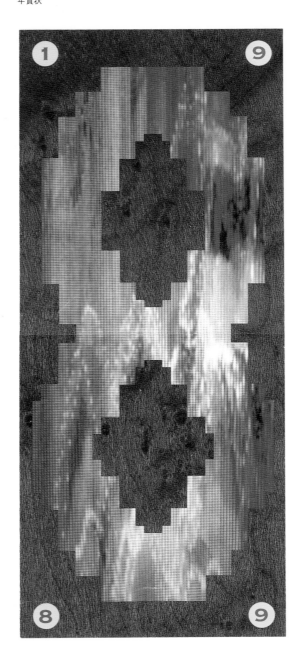

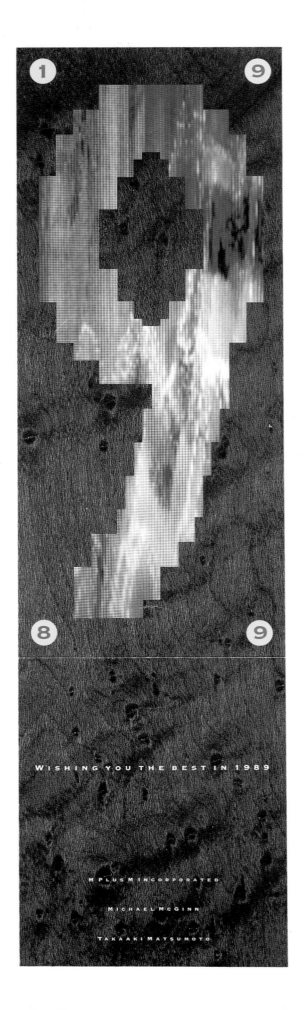

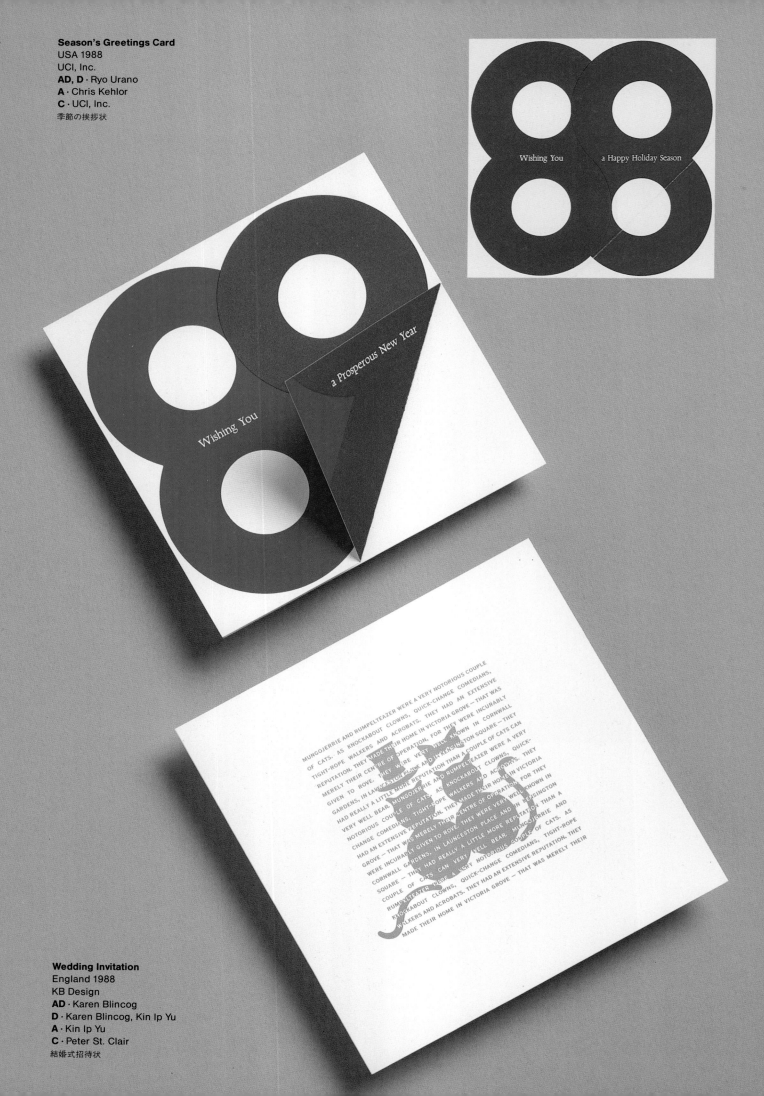

14   **Season's Greetings Card**
USA 1988
UCI, Inc.
AD, D · Ryo Urano
A · Chris Kehlor
C · UCI, Inc.
季節の挨拶状
結婚式招待状

14   **Wedding Invitation Card**
England 1988
KB Design
AD · Karen Blincog
D · Karen Blincog, Kin Ip Yu
A · Kin Ip Yu
C · Peter St. Clair
結婚式招待状

Christmas Card
Design/Planning office
Japan 1987
Douglas Design Office
AD, D · Douglas Doolittle
C · I.D. Corporation
クリスマスカード
デザイン／企画事務所

Moving Announcement
Design/Planning office
Japan 1988
Douglas Design Office
AD, D · Douglas Doolittle
C · I.D. Corporation
移転通知状
デザイン／企画事務所

16   **Christmas Card**
USA 1982
The Weller Institute for the Cure
of Design, Inc.
AD, D, A · Don Weller
C · Sun Graphics
クリスマスカード
グラフィックデザイン会社

New Year's Card
Graphic design firm
USA 1988
Follis Design
AD, D · John Follis
C · Follis Design
年賀状
グラフィックデザイン会社

ntina 1987
el Higa Diseno y
unicación Visual
D, A · Daniel Higa
Monica & Juan Carlos Higa
式招待状
(の米が入っている)

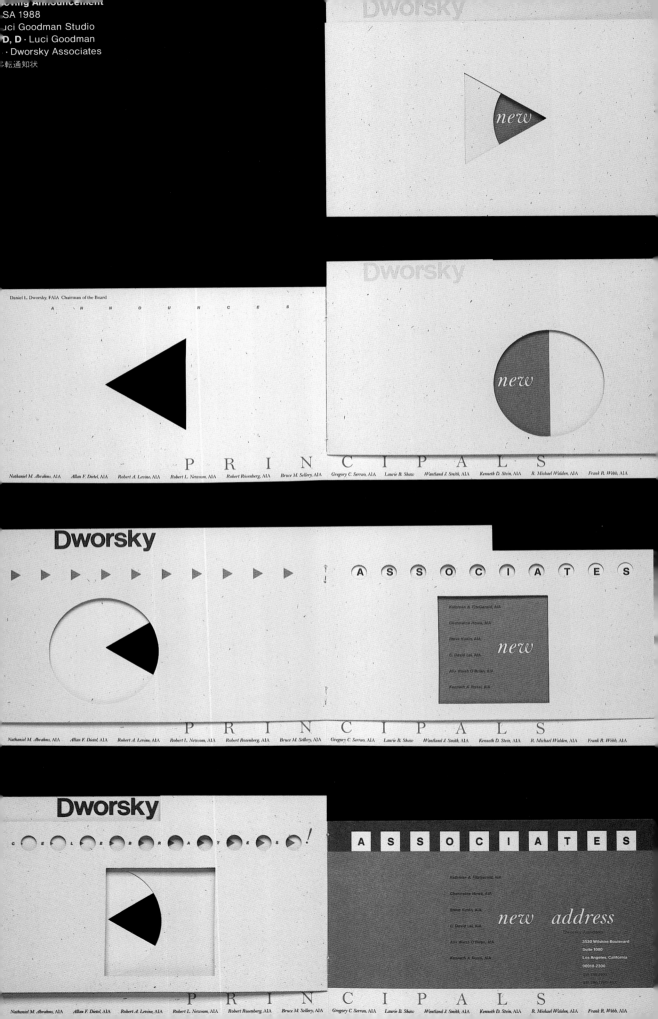

Wedding Invitation
Hong Kong 1988
Kan Tai-keung Design &
Associates Ltd.
AD, D · Freeman Lau
C · Candiee & Yiu Kwai
結婚式招待状

20 **Moving Announcement**
Graphic design firm
England 1979
Trickett & Webb Ltd.
AD · Lynn Trickett, Brian Webb
D · Andrew Thomas
C · Trickett & Webb Ltd.
移転通知状
グラフィックデザイン会社

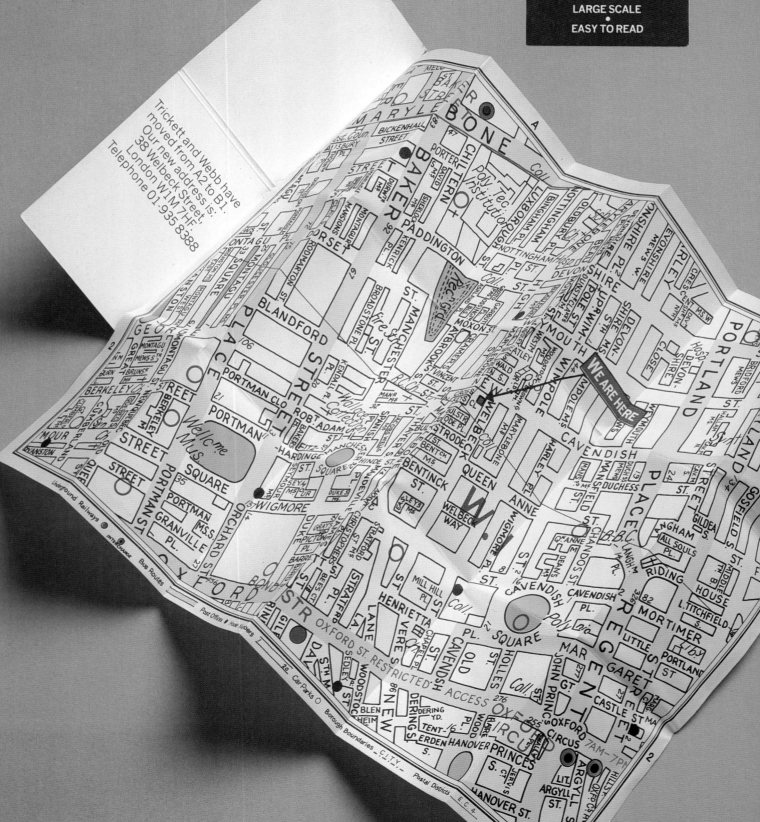

Postcard
Bar and restaurant
Australia 1987
Annette Harcus Design
AD, D, A · Annette Harcus
C · The Four In Hand
ポストカード
バー/レストラン

Christmas Card
USA 1984
Chermayeff & Geismar
Associates
AD, D, A · Ivan Chermayeff
C · American Artist Group
クリスマスカード

Season's Greetings Card
Graphic design firm
USA 1988
Pat Hansen Design
AD, D · Pat Hansen
C · Pat Hansen Design
季節の挨拶状
グラフィックデザイン会社

Opening Invitation
Australia 1986
Annette Harcus Design
AD, D, A · Annette Harcus
C · Blueberry Ash Square
オープニング招待状

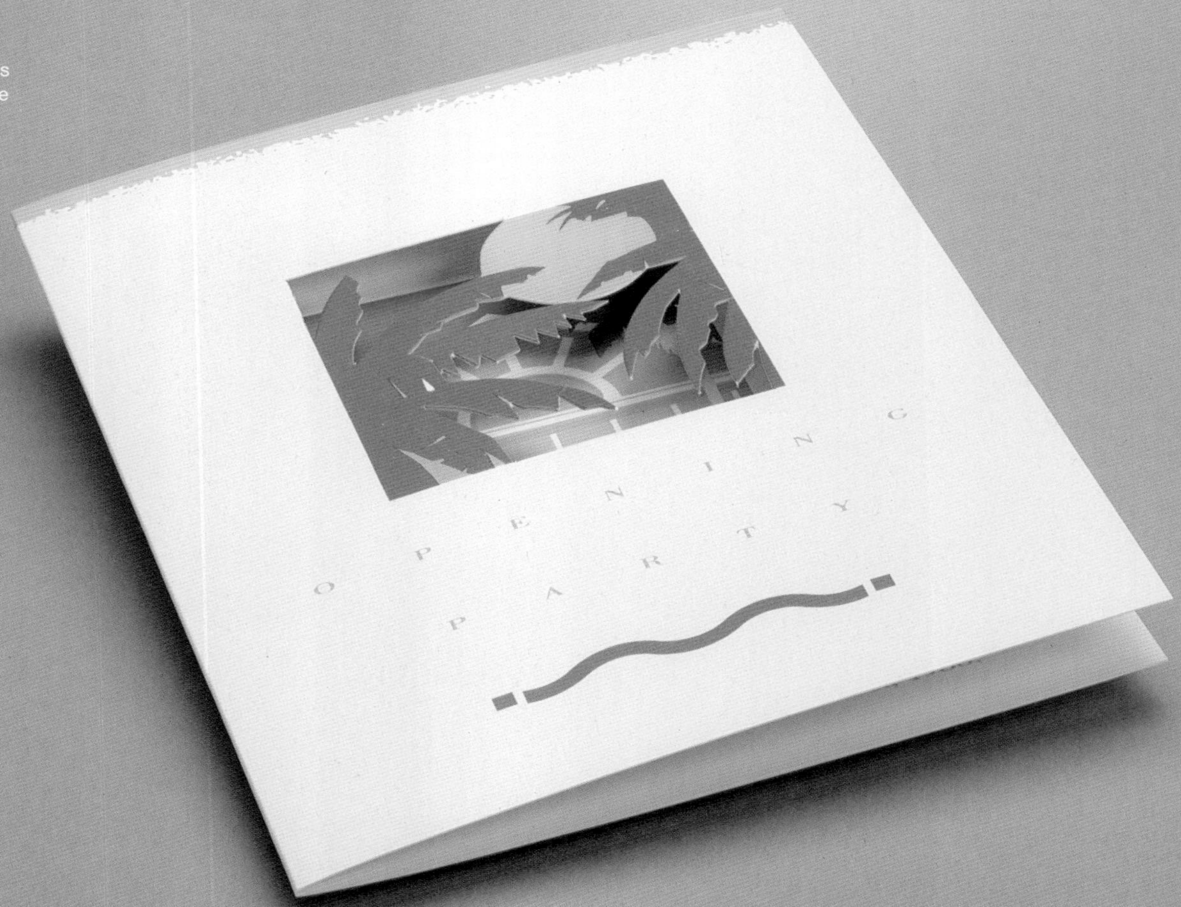

Wishing you a five-star holiday!

Pat Hansen Design

Wedding Invitation
Graphic designer
Hong Kong 1972
Kan Tai-keung Design &
Associates Ltd.
AD, D · Kan Tai-keung
C · Kan Tai-keung
結婚式招待状
グラフィックデザイナー

Moving Announcement
Graphic designer
USA 1986
Gina Federico
AD, D · Gina Federico
C · Gina Federico
移転通知状
グラフィックデザイナー

Change
of a
dress.

71 Park Place
New Canaan
Connecticut
06840

Gina Federico
graphic designer

203.966.7603

Season's Greetings Card
Graphic design firm
USA 1986
Louis Nelson Associates Inc.
AD · Louis Nelson
D · L. Nelson, D. O'Keefe
C · Louis Nelson Associates Inc.
季節の挨拶状
グラフィックデザイン会社

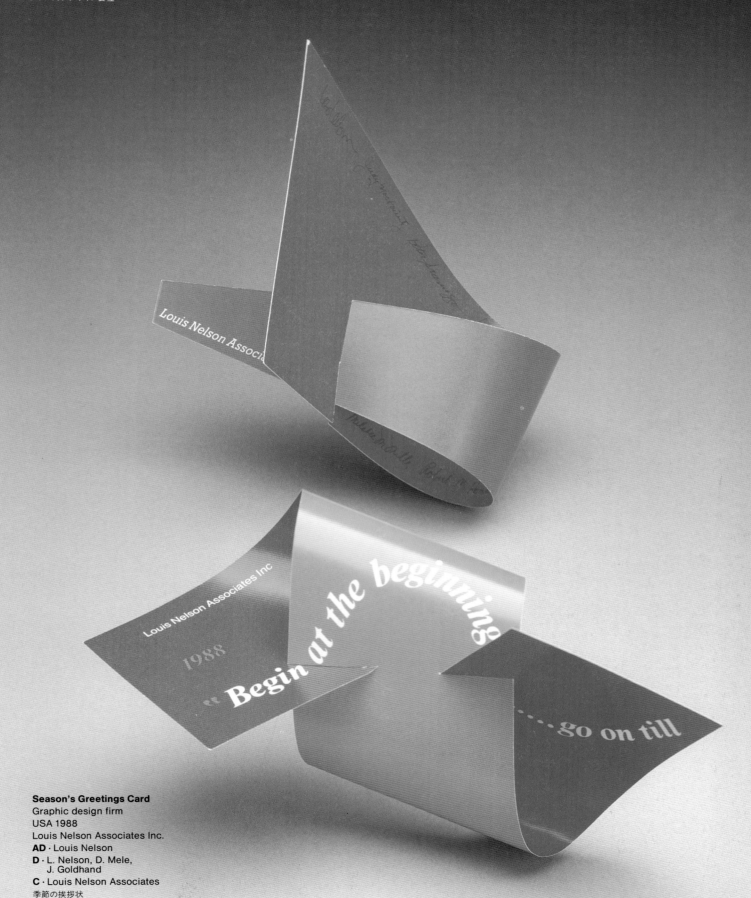

Season's Greetings Card
Graphic design firm
USA 1988
Louis Nelson Associates Inc.
AD · Louis Nelson
D · L. Nelson, D. Mele,
    J. Goldhand
C · Louis Nelson Associates
季節の挨拶状
グラフィックデザイン会社

26

Hanukkah Greeting Card
Graphic designer
USA
Lipson Alport Glass &
Associates
AD, D · Stan Brod
C · Stan Brod
ハヌカーの挨拶状
グラフィックデザイナー
（ハヌカーはユダヤ教の行事）

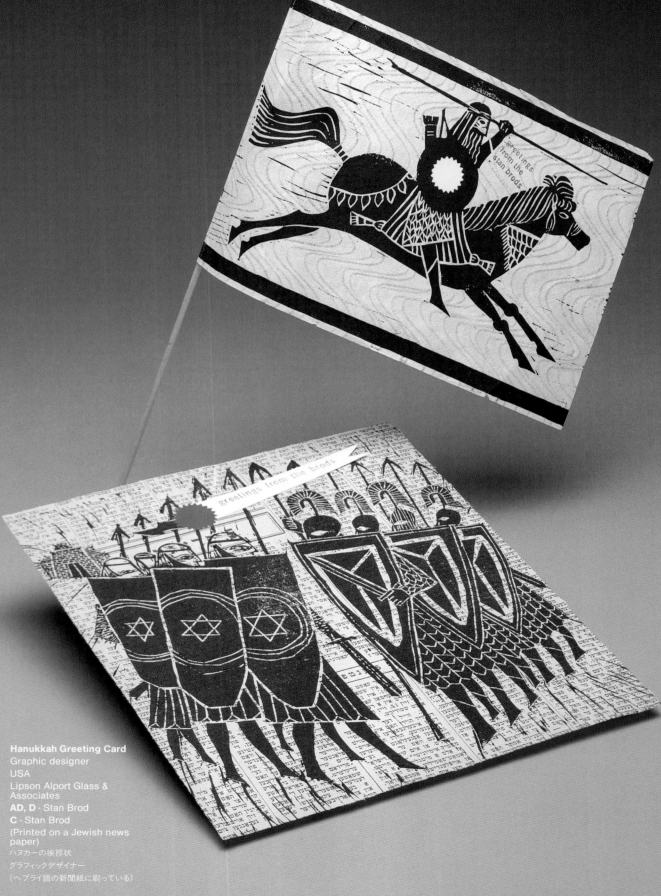

Hanukkah Greeting Card
Graphic designer
USA
Lipson Alport Glass &
Associates
AD, D · Stan Brod
C · Stan Brod
(Printed on a Jewish news
paper)
ハヌカーの挨拶状
グラフィックデザイナー
（ヘブライ語の新聞紙に刷っている）

Season's Greetings Card
Management consulting
company
Japan 1988
Inayoshi Design Inc.
AD, D · Hiromi Inayoshi,
  Miha Takagi
A · Jean-Michael Folon
C · Work Brain Inc.
季節の挨拶状
経営コンサルティング会社

Christmas Card
Graphic designer
USA 1972
David Leigh
AD, D, A · David Leigh
C · David Leigh
クリスマスカード
グラフィックデザイナー

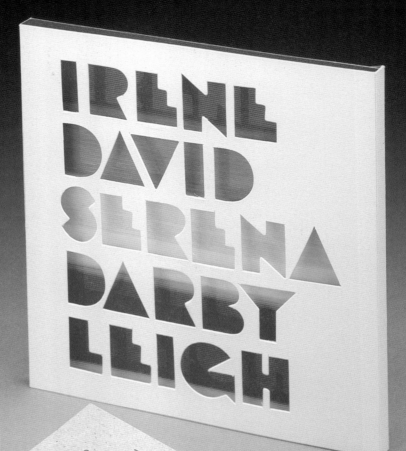

Auction Invitation
USA 1988
Concrete
AD · Jilly Simons
D · David Robson
A · David Csicsko
C · The Better Boys Foundation
オークション招待状

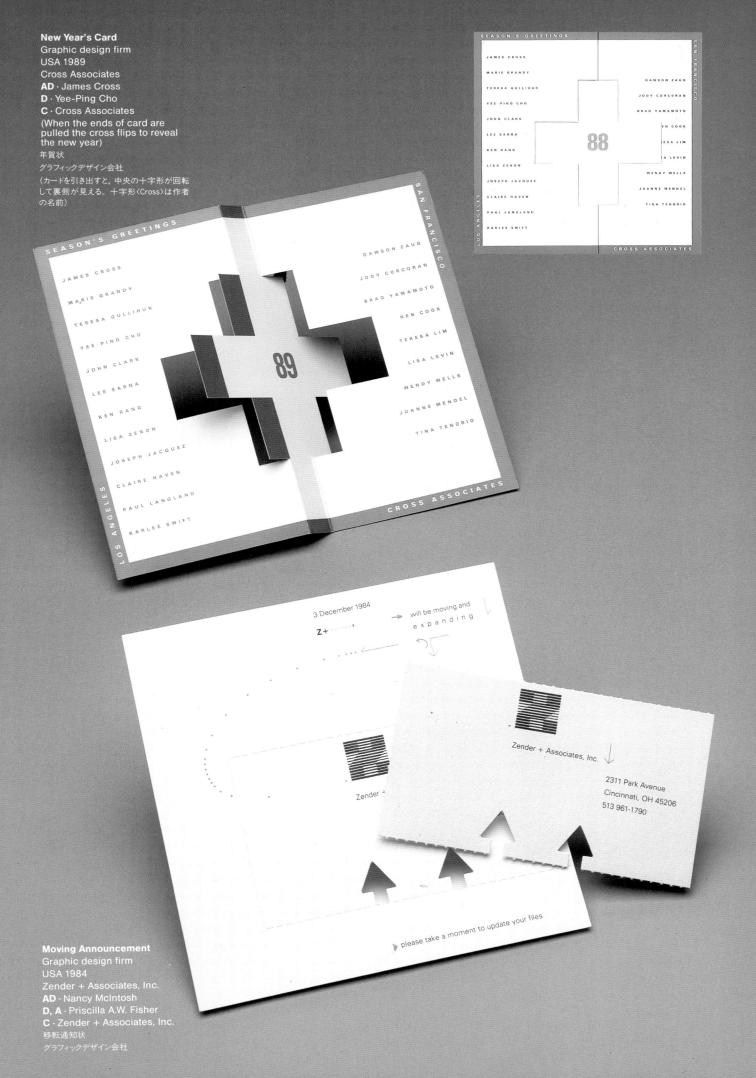

New Year's Card
Graphic design firm
USA 1989
Cross Associates
AD · James Cross
D · Yee-Ping Cho
C · Cross Associates
(When the ends of card are
pulled the cross flips to reveal
the new year)
年賀状
グラフィックデザイン会社
(カードを引き出すと，中央の十字形が回転
して裏側が見える。十字形〈Cross〉は作者
の名前)

SEASON'S GREETINGS

JAMES CROSS
MARIE GRANDY
TERESA GULLIHUR
YEE-PING CHO
JOHN CLARK
LEE SARNA
KEN RANG
LISA ZENON
JOSEPH JACQUEZ
CLAIRE HAVEN
PAUL LANGLAND
KARLEE SWIFT

DAWSON ZAUG
JODY CORCORAN
BRAD YAMAMOTO
KEN COOK
TERESA LIM
LISA LEVIN
WENDY WELLS
JOANNE MENDEL
TINA TENORIO

89

LOS ANGELES

SAN FRANCISCO

CROSS ASSOCIATES

SEASON'S GREETINGS

JAMES CROSS
MARIE GRANDY
TERESA GULLIHUR
YEE-PING CHO
JOHN CLARK
LEE SARNA
KEN RANG
LISA ZENON
JOSEPH JACQUEZ
CLAIRE HAVEN
PAUL LANGLAND
KARLEE SWIFT

DAWSON ZAUG
JODY CORCORAN
BRAD YAMAMOTO
KEN COOK
TERESA LIM
LISA LEVIN
WENDY WELLS
JOANNE MENDEL
TINA TENORIO

88

LOS ANGELES

SAN FRANCISCO

CROSS ASSOCIATES

3 December 1984

will be moving and
e x p a n d i n g

Z+

Zender + Associates, Inc.

2311 Park Avenue
Cincinnati, OH 45206
513 961-1790

please take a moment to update your files

Moving Announcement
Graphic design firm
USA 1984
Zender + Associates, Inc.
AD · Nancy McIntosh
D, A · Priscilla A.W. Fisher
C · Zender + Associates, Inc.
移転通知状
グラフィックデザイン会社

Christmas Cards
Chemical company
Italy 1986
Gottschalk + Ash International
AD · Gottschalk + Ash
International
D · Fritz Gottschalk,
Frederic Burbach
C · EniChem
クリスマスカード
化学製品会社

Season's Greetings Card
USA 1987
The Design Office of Wong & Yeo
AD, D, A · Hock Wah Yeo
C · The Kenwood Group
季節の挨拶状

Season's Greetings Card
Graphic design firm
India 1980
Desilva Associates
AD, D, A · Roby J.F. D'Silva
C · Desilva Associates
季節の挨拶状
グラフィックデザイン会社

32 **New Year's Card**
Graphic designer
Canada 1980
Eskind Waddell
AD · Malcolm Waddell
D · Brian Tsang
C · Eskind Waddell
年賀状
グラフィックデザイナー

And Peace to all,

From
Eskind Waddell

Season's Greetings Card
Graphic designer
Canada 1979
Eskind Waddell
AD · Malcolm Waddell
D · Leah Toby Hoffmitz
C · Eskind Waddell
季節の挨拶状
グラフィックデザイナー

Season's Greetings Card
Discotheque
Hong Kong 1985
Alan Chan Design Co.
AD · Alan Chan
D · Alan Chan, Alvin Chan,
　　Phillip Leung
C · Taipan Club Asia Ltd.
季節の挨拶状
ディスコ

Christmas Card
Graphic design firm
USA 1987
Zender + Associates, Inc.
AD, D, A · Priscilla A.W. Fisher
C · Zender + Associates, Inc.
クリスマスカード
グラフィックデザイン会社

Christmas Card
Graphic design firm
USA 1987
Zender + Associates, Inc.
AD, D, A · Priscilla A.W. Fisher
C · Zender + Associates, Inc.

Christmas Card
Hotel
USA 1987
de Harak & Poulin Associates
AD · Richard Poulin
D · Ran Van Koten
C · United Nations Plaza Hotel
クリスマスカード
ホテル

Invitation Card
USA 1988
UCSF Publications
AD, D, A · Vita Otrubova
C · The Chancellor's Office
招待状

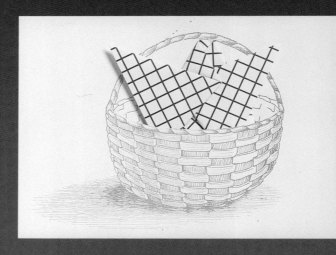

Pat and Julie Krevans
invite the members of Faculty Wives and their guests
to celebrate the coming of spring
at an indoor picnic
on Saturday, March 12, 1988
7:00 P.M.
The Chancellor's Residence

Valet Parking
Reply card and map enclosed

Picnic Baskets Galore
Plenty of seating . . . on the floor

Season's Greetings Card
USA 1986
Traci O'Very Covey
AD · Steve Grigg
D, A · Traci O'Very Covey
C · Cole & Weber Advertising
(Both sides of the same card)
季節の挨拶状
（一枚のカードの表と裏）

40 Wedding Invitation
Hong Kong 1988
Kan Tai-keung Design &
Associates Ltd.
AD · Kan Tai-keung
D · Freeman Lau
C · Terasa & Kenny Bee
結婚式招待状

New Year's Card
Graphic design firm
Hong Kong 1982
Graphic Communication Ltd.
AD, D · Henry Steiner
C · Graphic Communication Ltd.
年賀状
グラフィックデザイン会社
（戌年の年賀状）

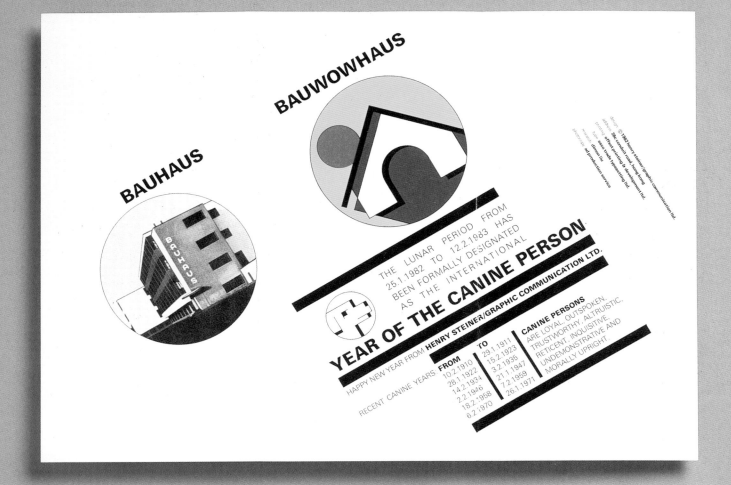

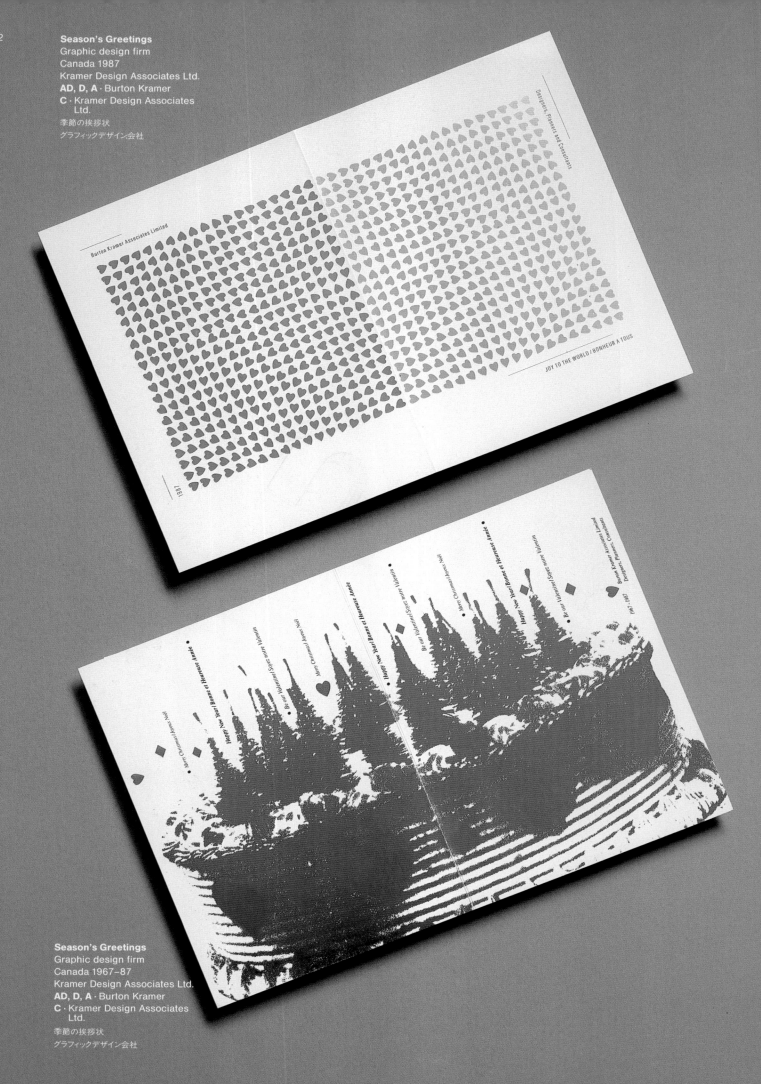

42 **Season's Greetings**
Graphic design firm
Canada 1987
Kramer Design Associates Ltd.
AD, D, A · Burton Kramer
C · Kramer Design Associates
Ltd.
季節の挨拶状
グラフィックデザイン会社

Season's Greetings
Graphic design firm
Canada 1967–87
Kramer Design Associates Ltd.
AD, D, A · Burton Kramer
C · Kramer Design Associates
Ltd.
季節の挨拶状
グラフィックデザイン会社

Graphic designer
Japan 1985
AD, D, A · Ross McBride
C · Ross McBride
Made by an American designer
in Japan to send to his friends
back home)

季節の挨拶状
グラフィックデザイナー
、日本に住むアメリカ人のデザイナーがアメ
リカの友人にあてたもの）

From the
Land of
the Rising
Sun,...

SEASON'S
GREETINGS

SEASON'S
GREETINGS

**Theater's 25th Anniversary
Party Invitation**
USA 1987
Pat Hansen
AD · Pat Hansen
D · Jesse Doquilo, Pat Hansen,
Bruce Hale
A · Pat Hansen, Bruce Hale
C · Seattle Repertory Theatre
劇場25周年パーティ招待状

Christmas Card
USA 1988
White + Associates
AD, D · White + Associates
C · White + Associates
クリスマスカード

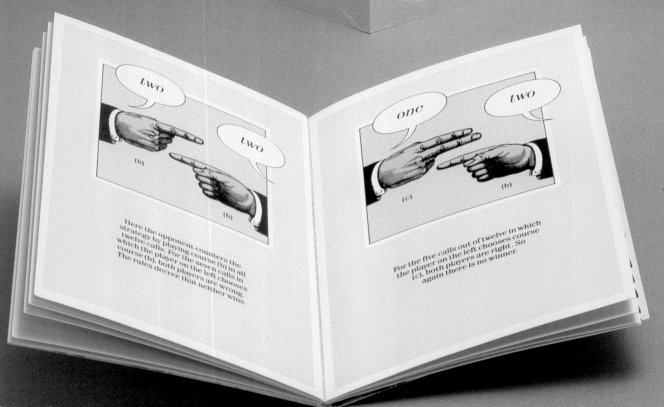

White-tailed Deer

White-footed Lemur

Chester White Boar

Here the opponent counters the strategy by playing course (b) in all twelve calls. For the seven calls in which the player on the left chooses course (b), both players are wrong. The rules decree that neither wins.

For the five calls out of twelve in which the player on the left chooses course (c), both players are right. So again there is no winner.

Christmas Greetings
Graphic design firm
England 1982
Pentagram Design Ltd.
AD · Mervyn Kurlansky
D · Mervyn Kurlansky,
   Paul Vickers
C · Pentagram Design Ltd.
(Booklet explains rules to an ancient hand game: "Mora")
クリスマスカード
グラフィックデザイン会社
（古くから伝わる手遊びを図説した小冊子）

Christmas Card
Graphic design firm
USA 1988
Richardson Smith Inc.
AD · Michael Westcott
D · Kun. Tee Chang
C · Richardson Smith Inc.
クリスマスカード
グラフィックデザイン会社

48

Opening Invitation
Pharmacy
Netherlands 1985
Frans Lieshout
AD, D · Frans Lieshout
C · Stichting Ka Geki
オープニング招待状
薬局

New Year's Card
Graphic designer
Switzerland 1980
Louis Mermet
AD, A · Luois Mermet
C · Louis Mermet
年賀状
グラフィックデザイナー

Chinese New Year's Party Invitation
Nightclub
Australia 1987
Flett Henderson & Arnold
AD · Richard Henderson
D, A · Flett Henderson & Arnold
C · Monsoon's Nightclub
中国式年賀パーティ招待状
ナイトクラブ

You are invited to celebrate Chinese New Year in true oriental style at Monsoon's Nightclub.

On Chinese New Year the colourful dragon will wind its way through the crowd. It is a time to celebrate happiness, health and good fortune.

Members and three guests - no charge.

Temporary Membership $10.

Date: Thursday, January 29, 1987
Time: 9.00pm

Moving Announcement
Design firm
Canada 1982
Rushton, Green and Grossutti Inc.
AD · Marc Grossutti
D · Sandra Kennedy
A · Marc Grossutti
C · Keith Rushton & Associates
移転通知状
デザイン会社

New Year's Card
Graphic designer
Norway 1987
Enzo Finger
AD, D · Enzo Finger
C · Enzo Finger
(Made of 2 cm thick plaster)
年賀状　　。
グラフィックデザイナー
（厚さ2センチの石膏で作られている）

Bare det beste og et godt Nyttår
Nur das Beste für das kommende Jahr
Tanti auguri per un felice anno nuovo

MCMLXXXVII

Enzo Finger, Designer ASG/Atypl/NGD
Skogryggvelen 7B, 0389 Oslo 3, Norway

Moving Announcement
Venture capital company
USA 1986
Carron Design
AD · Ross Carron
D · Ross Carron, Joann Maass
C · Walden
移転通知状
投資会社

Season's Greetings Card
Graphic design firm
USA 1987
Weisz Yang Dunkelberger Inc.
AD · Larry Yang
D · Bernard Reynoso
C · Weisz Dunkelberger Inc.
季節の挨拶状
グラフィックデザイン会社

New Year's Card
Graphic designer
Norway 1986
Enzo Finger
AD, D · Enzo Finger
C · Enzo Finger
年賀状
グラフィックデザイナー

Takk for det gamle & godt Nytt år!
All the Best & a happy New Year!
Auguri per un felice Anno Nuovo!
Die besten Wünsche
und ein gutes neues Jahr!

Enzo Finger, Designer ASG/A typit.
Skogryggsvn. 7 B, N 0389 Oslo 3.

Hanukkah 5732

Ruth, Stan, Deb, Dan and Mike Brod

Hanukkah Greeting Card
Graphic designer
USA
Lipson Alport Glass &
Associates
AD, D · Stan Brod
C · Stan Brod
ハヌカーの挨拶状
グラフィックデザイナー
（ハヌカーはユダヤ教の行事）

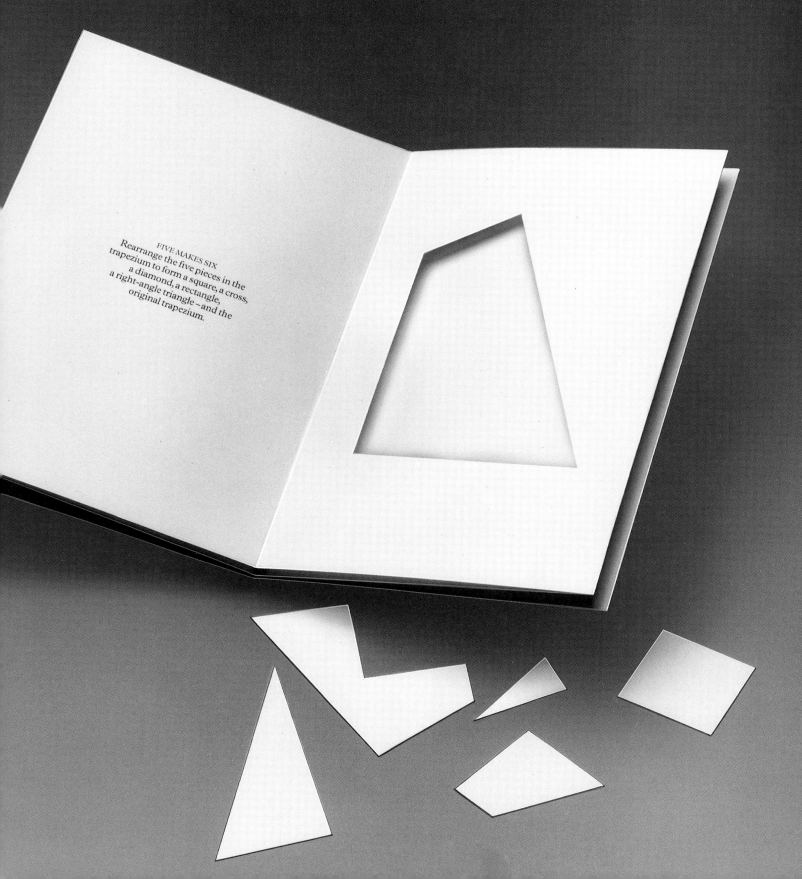

Christmas Greetings
Graphic design firm
England 1986
Pentagram Design Ltd.
AD · David Hillman
D · David Hillman, Amanda
   Bennett
C · Pentagram Design Ltd.
(Booklet comprised of six paper
puzzles)
クリスマスカード
グラフィックデザイン会社
（6種類のペーパー・パズルが入った小冊
子タイプのカード）

FIVE MAKES SIX
Rearrange the five pieces in the
trapezium to form a square, a cross,
a diamond, a rectangle,
a right-angle triangle – and the
original trapezium.

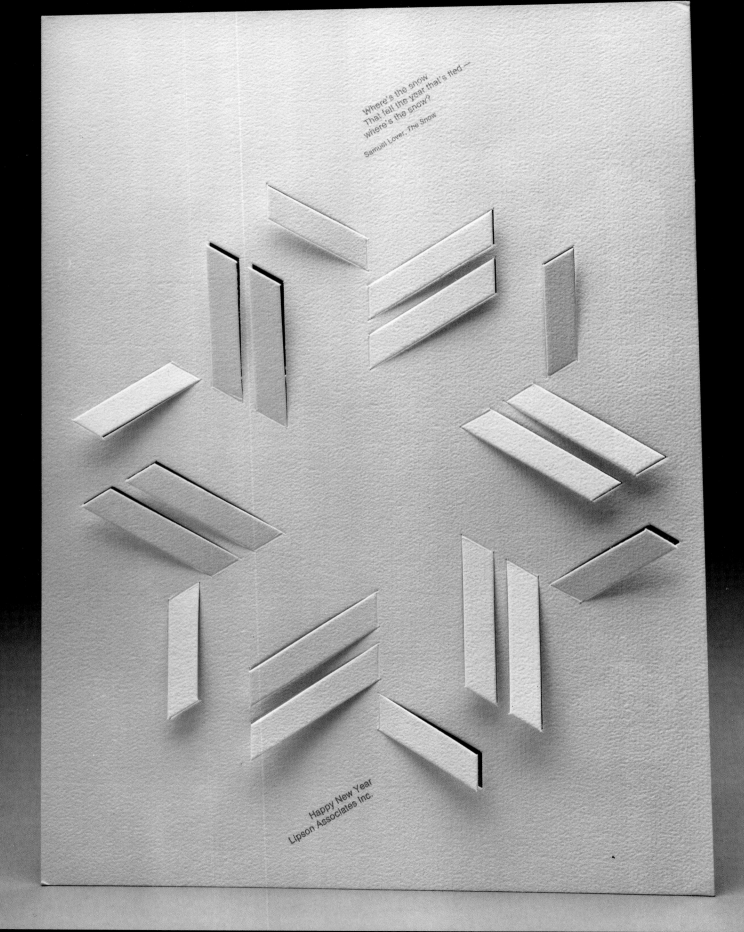

Where's the snow
That fell the year that's fled —
where's the snow?

Samuel Lover, The Snow

Happy New Year
Lipson Associates Inc.

Greetings Card
USA 1983
Murrie-White, Drummond,
Lienhart & Associates
AD, D · Jim Lienhart
A · Lin Eagle
C · California Dreamers, Inc.
挨拶状

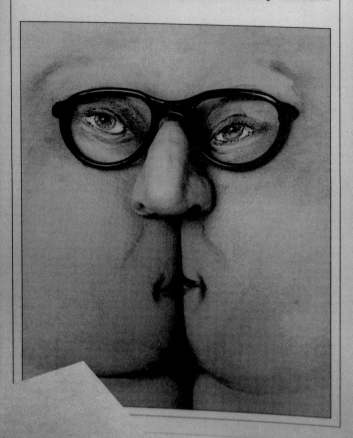

I've made an ass of myself so many times...

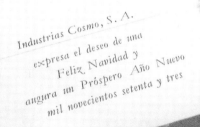

Industrias Cosmo, S.A.
expresa el deseo de una
Feliz Navidad y
augura un Próspero Año Nuevo
mil novecientos setenta y tres

Christmas Card
Record company
Spain 1973
Estudio Pla-Narbona
AD, D, A · Pla-Narbona
C · Industrias Cosmo, S.A.
クリスマスカード
レコード・プレーヤー製作会社

News agency
Switzerland 1988
Gottschalk + Ash International
AD · Gottschalk + Ash
　　International
D · Fritz Gottschalk, Hans Brandt
C · Reuters S.A.
季節の挨拶状
通信社

Invitation and Menu Card
40th year wedding anniversary
Netherlands 1987
Samenwerkende Ontwerpers
AD, D · André Toet
A · F. Depero
C · Els and Jan Vos
パーティ招待状/メニューカード
結婚40周年

1947 1987

Season's Greetings Card
Secours Populaire Français
France 1985
Grapus
AD, D, A · Grapus
C · Secours Populaire Français
季節の挨拶状
フランス民間救援センター

New Year's Card
Graphic design firm
France 1988
Visuel Design
AD, D · Jean Widmer
C · Visuel Design
年賀状
グラフィックデザイン会社

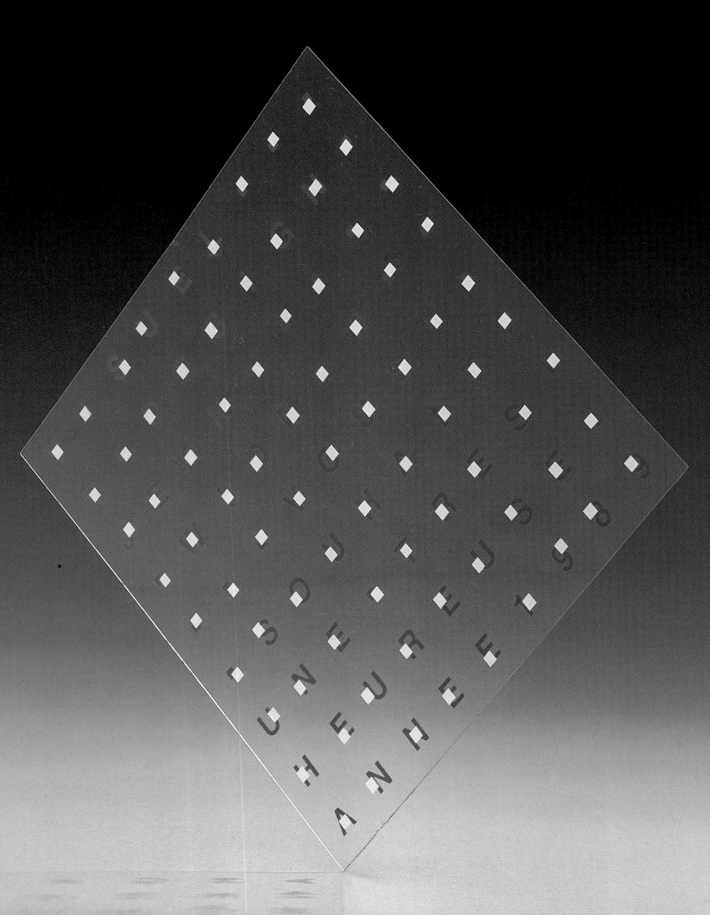

Exhibition Announcement
Switzerland 1972
BBV
AD, D · Michael Baviera
C · Art In Progress
展覧会案内状

15. Sept. bis 20. Okt. 1972

Christo

Retrospektive realisierter und
unrealisierter Projekte

Die Galerie
«art in progress»
möchte Sie zur Vernissage am
Freitag, 15. September 1972
18.00–20.00 einladen.
Der Künstler ist anwesend.

New Year's Cards
Package designer
Japan 1977, 82, 88
Yoshiko Kitagawa Design Studio
AD, D · Yoshiko Kitagawa
C · Yoshiko Kitagawa
年賀状
パッケージデザイナー

Postcard for a Couple
England 1987
Julia Alldridge Associates
AD, D, A · Julia Alldridge
C · Sarah Copplestone, David
　　Farmer
カップルのためのポストカード

You are cordially invited to
Audrey's
"Special" Birthday
Party

Wednesday 13 April 1988
Senior Common Room,
The Royal College of Art,
Kensington Gore, SW7
from 7.30 pm

Please
Not a word to Audrey

RSVP (in confidence) to
Sarah Copplestone, 7 Primrose Mews,
1A Sharpleshall Street, NW1 8YW
Tel: 01 483 2127

Birthday Party Invitation
England 1988
Julia Alldridge Associates
AD, D · Julia Alldridge
C · Sarah Copplestone
誕生日パーティ招待状

**Showroom Opening
Announcement**
USA 1987
Mark Anderson Design
AD · Mark Anderson
D, A · Earl Gee
C · The San Francisco Office
Pavilion
ショールーム・オープニング案内状

Blood Donor Card
Volunteer donor service
USA 1981
H.L. Chu & Company, Ltd.
AD, D · Hoi L. Chu
A · Ben Perez
C · NYU Medical Center Blood
　　Program
献血カード
献血奉仕組織

EAST

WEST

Concert Announcement
A concert of Chinese music for
Americans
USA 1988
The Design Office of Wong & Yeo
AD, D, A · Hock Wah Yeo
C · Asian Performing Arts
コンサート案内状
アメリカ人のための中国音楽コンサート

64

Office Opening Invitation
Chemical company
Canada 1988
Rushton, Green and Grossutti
Inc.
AD · Rushton, Green and
 Grossutti
D · Kirsti Ronback
C · DuPont Canada
オフィス・オープニング招待状
化学製品会社

DUPONT
CANADA

SHAPING THE FUTURE

You are cordially invited . . . .

The Board of Directors of the
Mississauga Civic Centre Art Gallery
cordially invites you to the Gala
Celebration of our First Anniversary.

Exbition Invitation
Art Galley
Canada 1988
Rushton, Green and Grossutti
Inc.
AD · Rushton, Green and
 Grossutti
D · Gino Ciarmela
C · Mississauga Civic Centre Art
 Gallery
展覧会招待状
アート・ギャラリー

Birth Announcement
USA 1988
Luci Goodman Studio
AD, D · Luci Goodman
C · David and Janet Mayes
誕生挨拶状

celebrate

the new additions to our lives

Through labor of love,

we have finished

the addition of a new

room to our home.

On September 12, 1988
David Vincent Mayes
7 pounds 6.5 ounces
and 21 inches in length
arrived at the wee hour
of 1:16 a.m. to the
delight of his parents
David and Janet Mayes.

Moving Announcement
England 1984
Trickett & Webb Ltd.
AD · Lynn Trickett, Brian Webb
D · Colin Sands
C · Trickett & Webb Ltd.
移転通知状

TRICKETT & WEBB
and
TRICKETT
ASSOCIATES
Have moved to

BLOOMSBURY

MARCHMONT ST

BLOOMSBURY
a
moving story

Christmas Cards
USA 1977
Crosby Associates Inc.
AD · Bart Crosby, Pat Crosby
D, A · Drew, Jill and Brad Crosby
C · The Crosby Family
39 from a set of 190 cards
(hand-made by the designer's
children)
クリスマスカード
デザイナーの子供たちが作った190点のう
ちの39点）

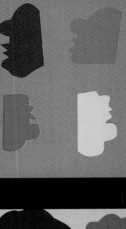

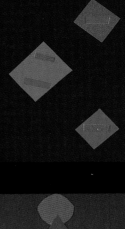
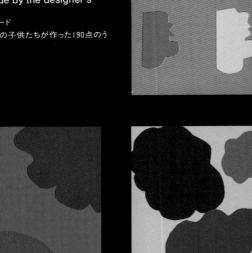

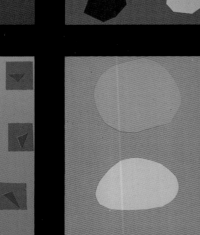

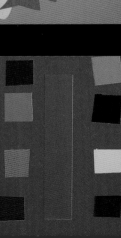

New Year's Card
West Germany 1988
Teunen & Teunen
AD, D · Jan Teunen
C · Teunen & Teunen
年賀状

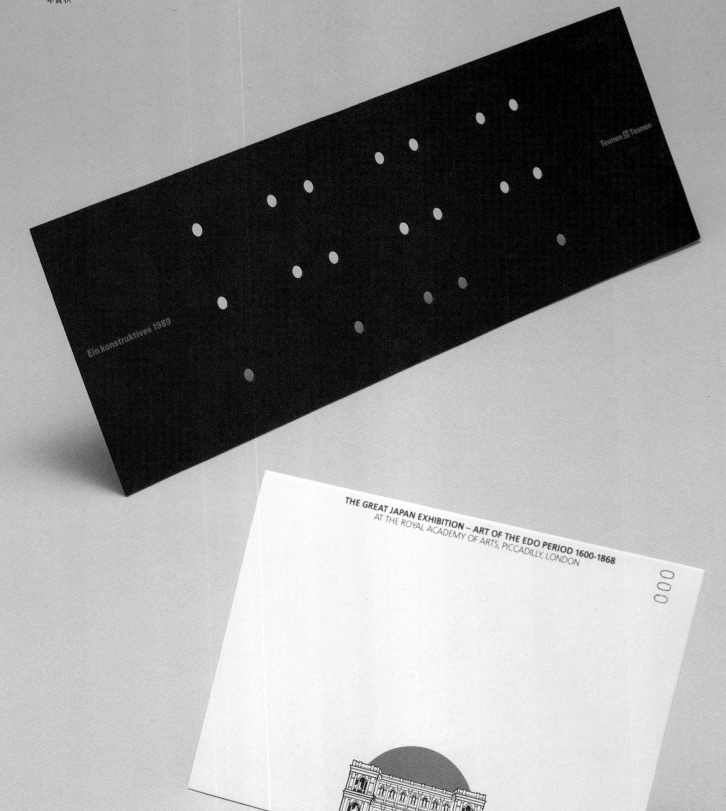

Exhibition Invitation
Japan exhibition
England 1981
Minale, Tattersfield and Partners
Ltd.
AD · Alex Maranzano
D, A · Dimitri Karavias
C · Sony (UK) Ltd.
日本展案内状

Season's Greetings Card
Graphic design firm
India 1984–85
Desilva Associates
AD, D, A · Roby J.F. D'Silva
C · Desilva Associates
季節の挨拶状
グラフィックデザイン会社
季節の挨拶状
グラフィックデザイン会社

Christmas Card
Graphic designer
USA 1970
David Leigh
AD, D, A · David Leigh
C · David Leigh
クリスマスカード
グラフィックデザイナー

Christmas Card
Museum
USA 1969
David Leigh
AD, D, A · David Leigh
C · The Museum of Modern Art,
New York
クリスマスカード
美術館

Christmas Card
Graphic designer
USA 1969
David Leigh
AD, D, A · David Leigh
C · David Leigh
クリスマスカード
グラフィックデザイナー

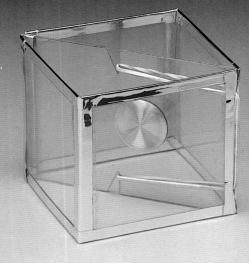

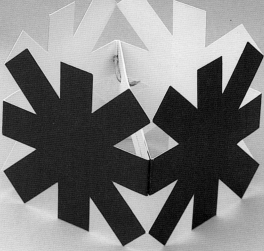

Christmas Card
Graphic designer
USA 1967
David Leigh
AD, D, A · David Leigh
C · David Leigh
クリスマスカード
グラフィックデザイナー

(Cards automatically pop-up
with rubber band action when
removed from the envelope)
（封筒から出すと自動的に立体になる。ゴ
ム・バンドが使われている）

Season's Greetings Cards
Graphic design firm
Netherlands 1983
Maarten Vijgenboom Design
AD, D, A · Maarten Vijgenboom
C · Maarten Vijgenboom
季節の挨拶状
グラフィックデザイン会社

ontwerpburo
maarten vijgenboom
venlo

prettige feestdagen

en een toost op
een sprankelend
gezond
gelukkig
voorspoedig
zalig
succesvol
te gek
fijn
nieuw
jaar

ontwerpburo
maarten vijgenboom
wenst u prettige feestdagen
en zorgt dat u ook in '88 door het bos
de boom nog ziet

Christmas Cards
Graphic design firm
England 1982–84
Trickett & Webb Ltd.
AD · Lynn Trickett, Brian Webb
D · Marion Dalley, Lynn Trickett,
Brian Webb, Ian Cockburn,
Sarah Mattinson
A · Marion Dalley,
Simon Browning,
Ian Cockburn,
Sarah Mattinson
C · Trickett & Webb Ltd.
(Actual badges attached)
クリスマスカード
グラフィックデザイン会社
（実際に使えるバッジが付いている）

Christmas Card
Graphic designer's family
USA 1981
G. Salchow Design
AD, D · Gordon Salchow
C · The Salchow Family
クリスマスカード
デザイナーの家族

Compliments Card
Telecommunications workshop
Netherlands 1987
Total Design bv
AD, D · Robert van Rixtel
C · PTT Centrale Werkplaats
挨拶状
通信ワークショップ

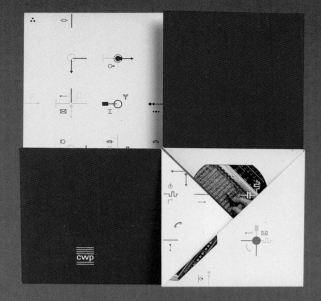

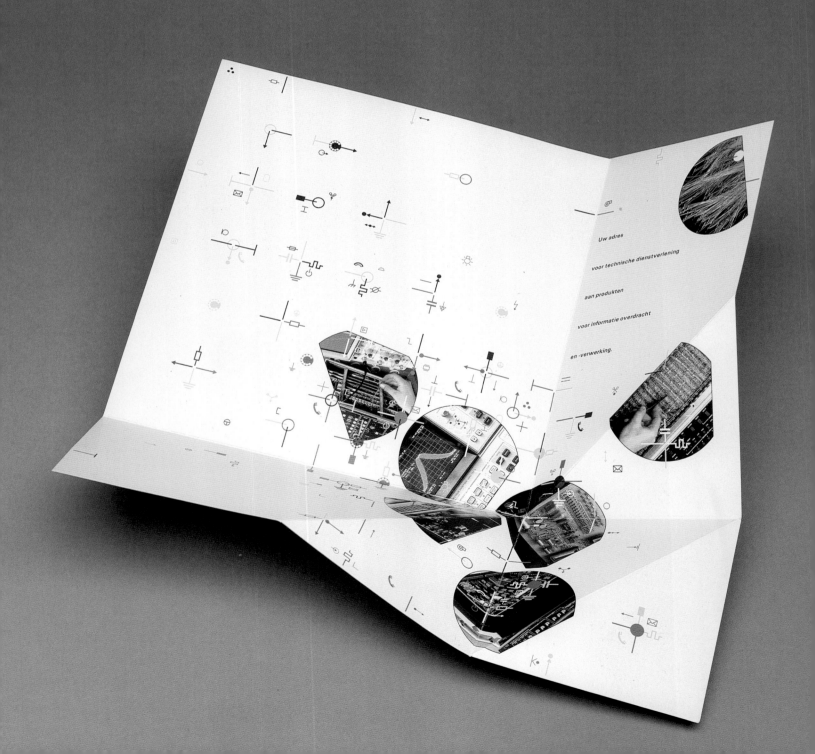

Christmas Card
Software company
USA 1987
Tandem Studios
AD, D, A · Daniel Ruesch
C · Novell, Inc.
クリスマスカード
ソフトウェア会社

Moving Announcement
Audio visual company
England 1983
Trickett & Webb Ltd.
AD · Lynn Trickett, Brian Webb
D · Lynn Trickett, Brian Webb,
Marion Dalley
C · The Visual Connection
(Comprised of a ball bearing
game)
移転通知状
オーディオ・ビジュアル会社
（実際に遊べるボールベアリング・ゲームが
付いている）

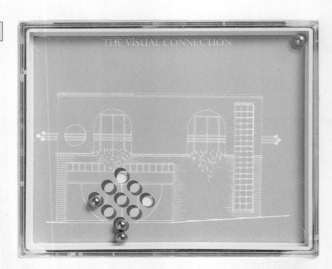

ON THE MOVE...........

our new address is:

THE VISUAL CONNECTION
1 Rostrevor Mews London SW6 5AZ Telephone 01-731 6300 Telex 995801 Ref V1

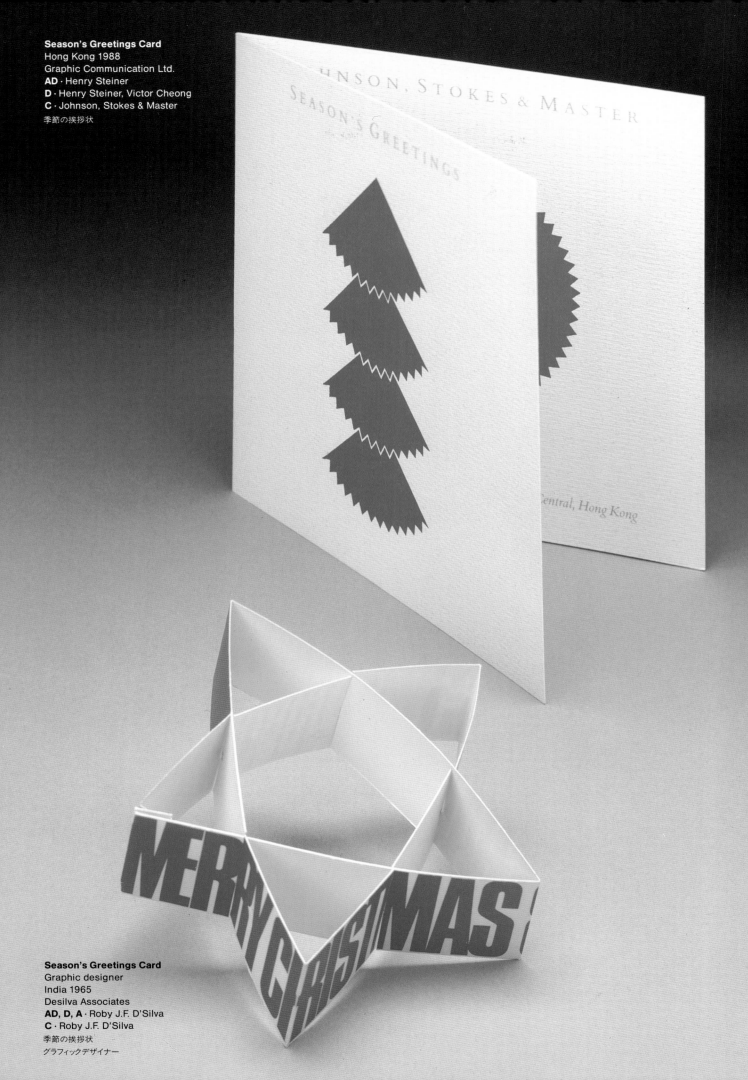

Season's Greetings Card
Hong Kong 1988
Graphic Communication Ltd.
AD · Henry Steiner
D · Henry Steiner, Victor Cheong
C · Johnson, Stokes & Master
季節の挨拶状

Season's Greetings Card
Graphic designer
India 1965
Desilva Associates
AD, D, A · Roby J.F. D'Silva
C · Roby J.F. D'Silva
季節の挨拶状
グラフィックデザイナー

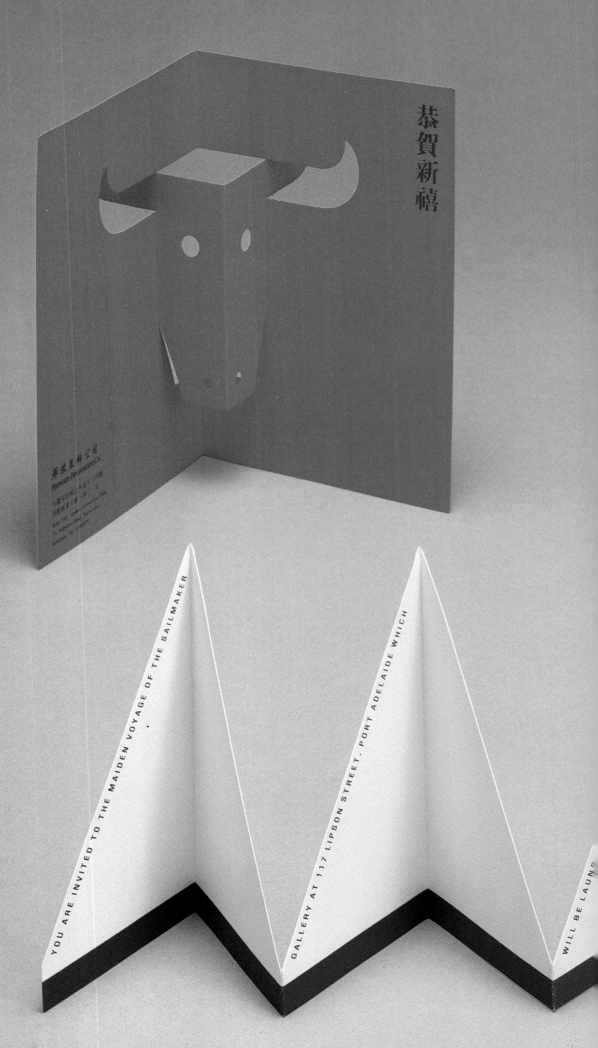

78

New Year's Card
Interior decorating company
Hong Kong 1985
Kan Tai-keung Design &
Associates Ltd.
AD · Kan Tai-keung
D · Dennis Lau
C · Famous Decoration Co.
年賀状
インテリア装飾会社

Opening Invitation
Art Gallery
Australia 1986
Barrie Tucker Design
AD · Barrie Tucker
D · Caz Tilly
C · The Sailmaker Gallery
オープニング招待状
アート・ギャラリー

Season's Greetings Card
Museum
USA 1988
Shimokochi/Reeves Design
AD · Mamoru Shimokochi,
　Anne Reeves
D · Mamoru Shimokochi
C · Museum of Contemporary Art
季節の挨拶状
美術館

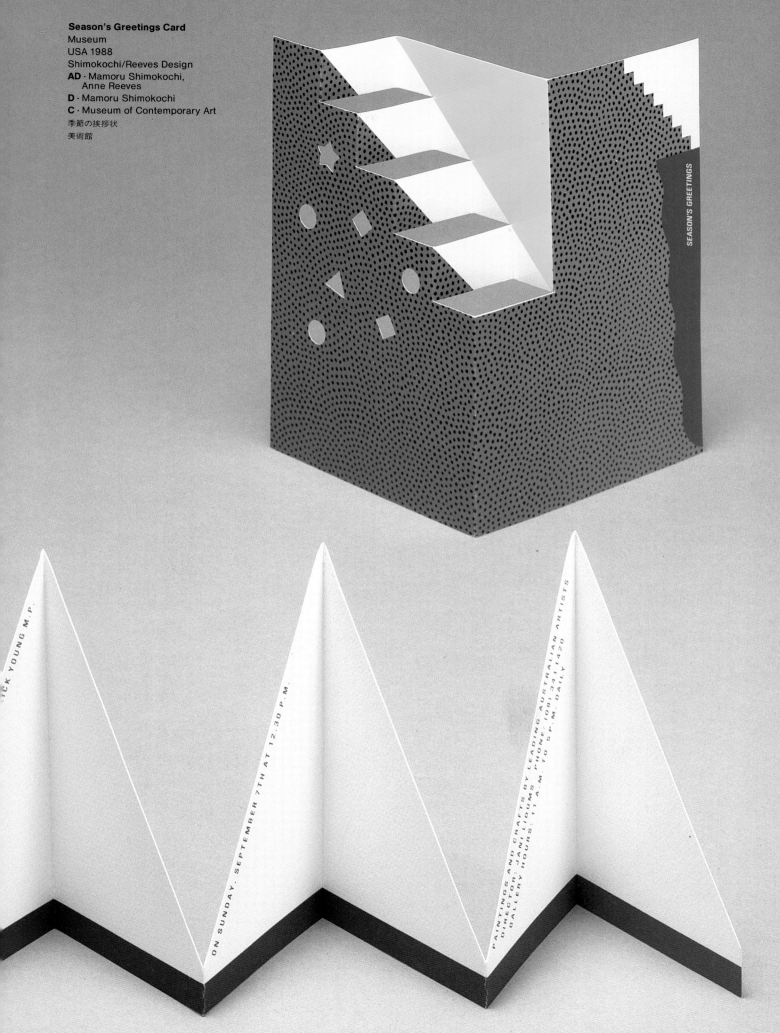

80

Christmas Card
Pharmaceutical company
Spain 1969
Estudio Pla-Narbona
AD, D, A · Pla-Narbona
C · J. Uriah & Cia, S.A.
クリスマスカード
製薬会社

Christmas Card
Designer's family
USA 1973
Crosby Associates Inc.
AD, D · Bart Crosby
A · Bart, Pat, Drew, Jill and
   Brad Crosby
C · The Crosby Family
クリスマスカード
デザイナーの家族

Invitation Card
USA 1983
Laughlin/Winkler
AD, D · Mark Laughlin,
Ellen Winkler
C · Boston Shakespeare Co.
招待状

a gala to celebrate

the lighthouse

a gala to celebrate

the lighthouse

saturday   5 november 1983

7 00   cocktails
8 00   dinner
9 00   performance
the american premiere of a short work
by peter maxwell davies
9 30   dessert buffet

the board of directors
and board of advisers
of boston shakespeare company
peter sellars, artistic director

invite you to attend a
gala evening
to celebrate the american premiere of
peter maxwell davies' the lighthouse

peter maxwell davies, guest of honor

hotel meridien
boston
black tie

**Change of Telephone Number
Announcement**
Graphic design firm
West Germany 1982
Mendell & Oberer
AD, D · Pierre Mendell
C · Mendell & Oberer
電話番号変更通知状
グラフィックデザイン会社

Season's Greetings Card
Greece
L. Katzouraki
AD, D · L. Katzouraki
C · L. Katzouraki
季節の挨拶状

Christmas Card
Graphic design firm
England 1976
Trickett & Webb Ltd.
AD · Lynn Trickett, Brian Webb
D · Andrew Thomas, Lynn
    Trickett, Brian Webb
A · Andrew Thomas
C · Trickett & Webb Ltd.
クリスマスカード
グラフィックデザイン会社

Christmas Card
Graphic design firm
England 1978
Trickett & Webb Ltd.
AD · Lynn Trickett, Brian Webb
D · Shaun Dew, Lynn Trickett,
    Brian Webb
A · Shaun Dew
C · Trickett & Webb Ltd.
クリスマスカード
グラフィックデザイン会社

84

Christmas Card
Australia 1987
Flett Henderson & Arnold
AD · Flett Henderson
D, A · Flett Henderson & Arnold
C · PA Consulting
クリスマスカード
清涼飲料会社

Christmas Card
Soft drinks company
Italy 1982
Minale, Tattersfield and Partners
Ltd.
AD · Marcello Minale
D, A · Ian Delaney
C · Fonti Levissima
クリスマスカード
清涼飲料会社

Invitation Card
USA 1988
Skolos Wedell + Raynor, Inc.
AD, D · Laura Silverman
C · Union Office Supply
招待状

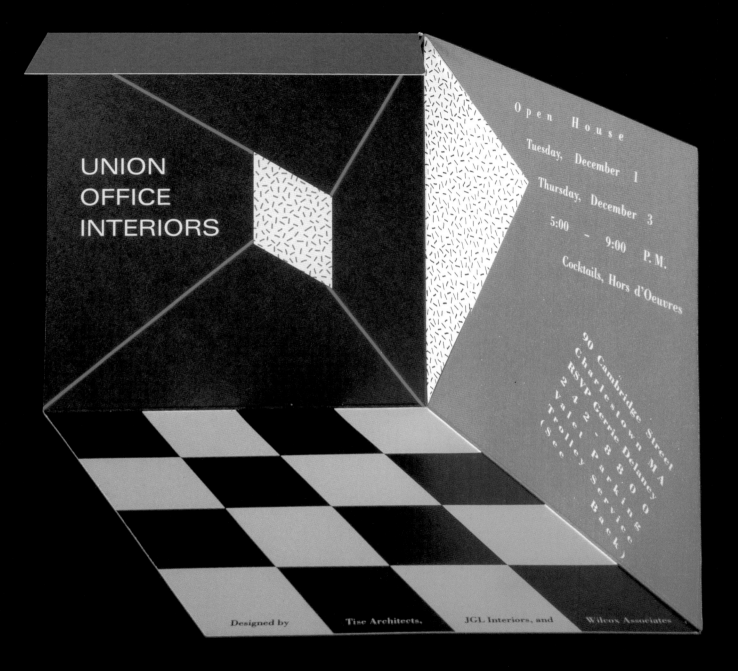

86 **Wedding Announcement**
Switzerland 1986
BBV
AD, D · Michael Baviera
C · Regula & Daniel Grunder
結婚式案内状

Season's Greetings Card
Graphic design firm
Argentina 1989
Shakespear Estudio de Diseño
AD, D · Shakespear Estudio de
Diseño
C · Shakespear Estudio de
Diseño
季節の挨拶状
グラフィックデザイン会社

'80–'86 New Year's Cards
Design firm
Japan 1979–85
Igarashi Studio
AD · Takenobu Igarashi
D · Igarashi Studio
C · Igarashi Studio
年賀状
デザイン会社

88 **Christmas Greetings**
Graphic design firm
England 1985
Pentagram Design Ltd.
AD · John McConnell
D · John McConnell, Thierry
Gogniat
C · Pentagram Design Ltd.
(Booklet introduces three award-
winning paper airplane designs,
and explains how to build them)
クリスマスカード
グラフィックデザイン会社
(紙飛行機コンテストで優勝した
飛行機の作り方を説明している)

Museum Opening Invitation
Canada 1988
Furman Graphic Design
AD, D · Neville Smith, Aviva
Furman
C · National Aviation Museum
美術館オープニング招待状

Christmas Card
Graphic designer
West Indies 1986
Russel Halfhide Graphic Design
AD, D, A · Russel Halhide
C · Russel Halfhide
(29.5cm×38.6cm)
クリスマスカード
グラフィックデザイナー
（作品は29.5cm×38.6cmの大きさ）

SEASON'S GREETINGS
RUSSEL HALFHIDE
GRAPHIC DESIGN

90

Moving Announcement
USA 1987
Sussman/Prejza
AD, D · Deborah Sussman
C · Hasbro, Inc.
移転通知状

HASBRO

Hasbro and its family

is relocating their New York City

Offices & S

M

O

Party Invitation
Graphic design firm
USA 1987
Sussman/Prejza
AD, D · Deborah Sussman
A · Francois Asselin
C · Sussman/Prejza
パーティ招待状
グラフィックデザイン会社

Sussman, Prejza & Company wishes you a happy holiday season and invites you and a guest to join us on Sunday December 20th from 7:30 pm to Midnight to enjoy food, drink,

V E · SO

32 West 23rd Street

effective, August 1986

New York, New York 10010 ☎ 212 645 2400

32 West 23rd

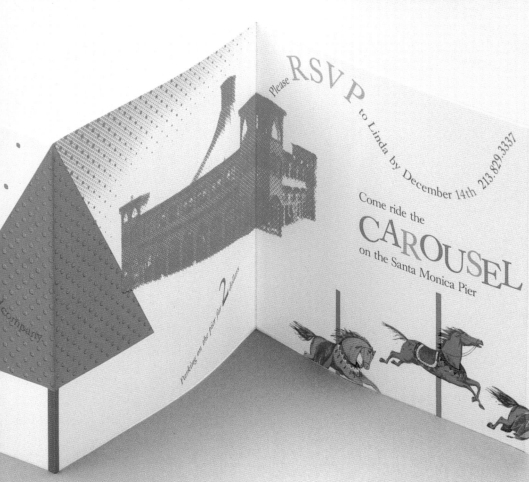

Please RSVP to Linda by December 14th 213.829.3337

Come ride the
CAROUSEL
on the Santa Monica Pier

Parking on the pier for 2 hours

...company

92 **Season's Greetings**
News agency
Switzerland 1988
Gottschalk + Ash International
AD · Gottschalk + Ash
　International
D · Fritz Gottschalk, Hans Brandt
C · Reuters S.A.
(An alternative package-type
greeting)
季節の挨拶状
通信社
（特別製のスタンプが入ったパッケージタイ
プのグリーティングカード）

Moving Announcement
Qualitative research
England 1987/88
Liz James Design Associates
AD · Liz James
D · Liz James, David Wood
C · Rachel Ormrod
移転通知状
マーケティング・リサーチ会社

RACHEL ORMROD
QUALITATIVE RESEARCH
22 EARLS COURT SQUARE
LONDON SW5 9DN
TELEPHONE 01·370 7885

RACHEL ORMROD
SPECIALISES IN STRATEGIC
AND CREATIVE DEVELOPMENT
OF PRODUCTS, BRANDS
AND ADVERTISING

94

Greeting Card
Graphic design firm
USA 1987
Mike Quon Design Office, Inc.
AD, D, A · Mike Quon
C · Mike Quon Design Office,
　　Inc.
挨拶状
グラフィックデザイン会社

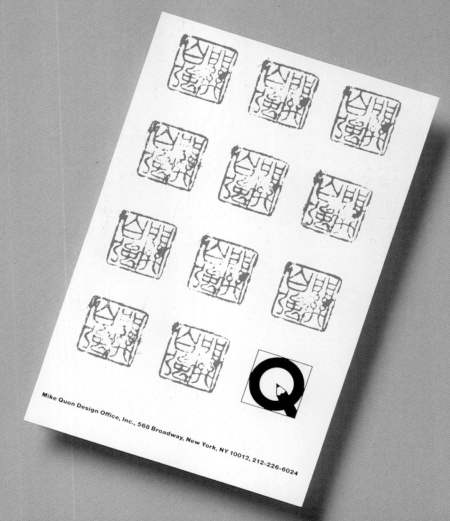

Moving Announcement
Graphic designer
USA 1988
Gina Federico Graphic Design
AD, D, A · Gina Federico
C · Gina Federico
移転通知状
グラフィックデザイナー

Season's Greetings Card
USA 1971
Anspach Grossman Portugal
AD · Eugene Grossman
D, A · Willi Kunz
C · Anspach Grossman Portugal
季節の挨拶状
グラフィックデザイン会社

Season's Greetings Card
Museum
USA 1979
H.L. Chu & Company, Ltd.
AD, D · Hoi L. Chu
A · Ben Perez
C · Museum of Modern Art,
  New York
季節の挨拶状
美術館

New Year's Card
Design firm
Hong Kong 1985
Kan Tai-keung Design &
Associates Ltd.
AD · Kan Tai-keung
D · Dennis Lau
C · SS Design & Production
年賀状
デザイン会社

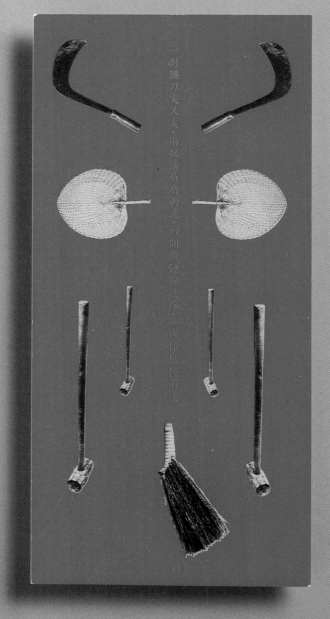

Business Announcement
USA 1980
Willi Kunz Associates Inc.
AD, D, A · Willi Kunz
C · Willi Kunz Associates Inc.
案内状

Season's Greetings Card
Graphic design firm
USA 1981
Willi Kunz Associates Inc.
AD, D, A · Willi Kunz
C · Willi Kunz Associates Inc.
季節の挨拶状
グラフィックデザイン会社

Season's Greetings Card
USA 1988
Willi Kunz Associates Inc.
AD, D, A · Willi Kunz
C · Willi Kunz Associates Inc.
季節の挨拶状

Moving Announcement
USA 1981
Willi Kunz Associates Inc.
AD, D, A · Willi Kunz
C · Willi Kunz Associates Inc.
移転通知状

Willi Kunz Associates Inc

SEASON'S GREETINGS

ENJOY

Willi Kunz Associates

Willi Kunz Associates Inc

Graphic Communications Design

2112 Broadway New York, NY 10023 212 799 4300

Willi Kunz Associates is expanding...

New address

New telephone

Christmas Card
Graphic design firm
USA 1988
Peter Walberg Design
AD, D, A · Peter Walberg
C · Peter and Jane Walberg
クリスマスカード
グラフィックデザイン会社

British Airports

Postcard
England 1972
Minale, Tattersfield and Partners
Ltd.
AD, D, A · Brian Tattersfield
C · British Airports Authority
ポストカード
ポストカードデザイン会社

New Year's Card
Graphic design firm
Japan 1988
Igarashi Studio
AD · Takenobu Igarashi
D · Noreen Fukumori
C · Igarashi Studio
年賀状
グラフィックデザイン会社

Business Announcement
Graphic design firm
Canada 1975
Eskind Waddell
AD · Roslyn Eskind
D · Malcolm Waddell
C · Eskind Waddell
案内状
グラフィックデザイン会社

Ballet Invitation
USA 1988
Zander + Associates, Inc.
AD, D, A · Mary Beth McSwigan
C · Cincinnati Ballet
バレー招待状

1988 ▼.▼.▼
Nutcracker
Ball

*An
Imperial
Russian
Fantasy*

Season's Greetings Card
Graphic design firm
India 1987
Desilva Associates
AD, D, A · Roby J.F. D'Silva
C · Desilva Associates
季節の挨拶状
グラフィックデザイン会社

Season's Greetings Card
France 1986
Grapus
AD, D, A · Grapus
C · Parc de la Villette
季節の挨拶状

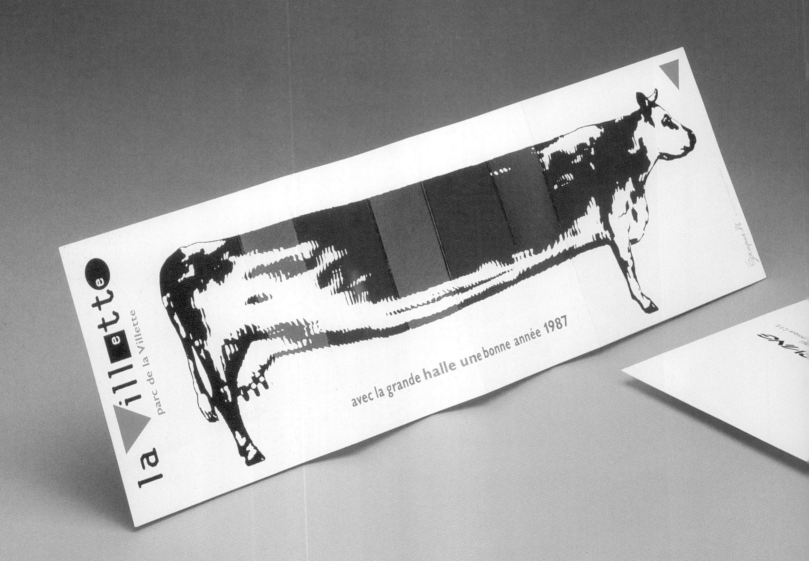

Invitation Card
Housing fair
France 1986
Grapus
AD, D, A · Grapus
C · Grapus
ハウジング・フェア招待状

du 7 au 15 mars 87
la grande halle, la Villette

la Villette   la grande halle

MEDIFA   présente   HABITER 87

la création à portée de la main

VIA   MOVING
une réalisation VIA, MOVING
réalisation technique C.F.E.

contact habiter 87 : 42 93 60 25
10 place sainte Opportune Paris 75001

Grapus 86

Postcard
Australia 1981
Cozzolino-Hughes
AD · Mimmo Cozzolino
D · Cozzolino-Hughes
A · Con Aslanis
C · Centre of Italian Studies,
　　Melbourne
ポストカード

New Year's Card
Hong Kong 1984
Kan Tai-keung Design &
Associates Ltd.
AD · Kan Tai-keung
D · Lee Liw Chee
C · Wardley Investment Services
　　Ltd.
年賀状

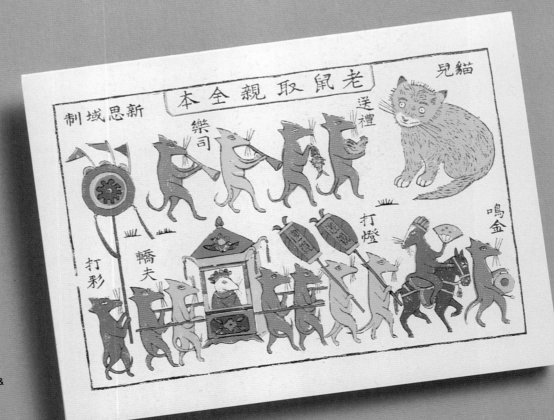

Exhibition Invitation
ISPAA Hong Kong Show
Hong Kong 1988
Kan Tai-keung Design &
Associates Ltd.
AD, D · Kan Tai-keung
C · The Hong Kong Institute for
Promotion of Chinese
Culture
展覧会招待状

Christmas Card
USA 1980
Mike Quon Design Office, Inc.
AD, D, A · Mike Quon
C · QuonArt
クリスマスカード

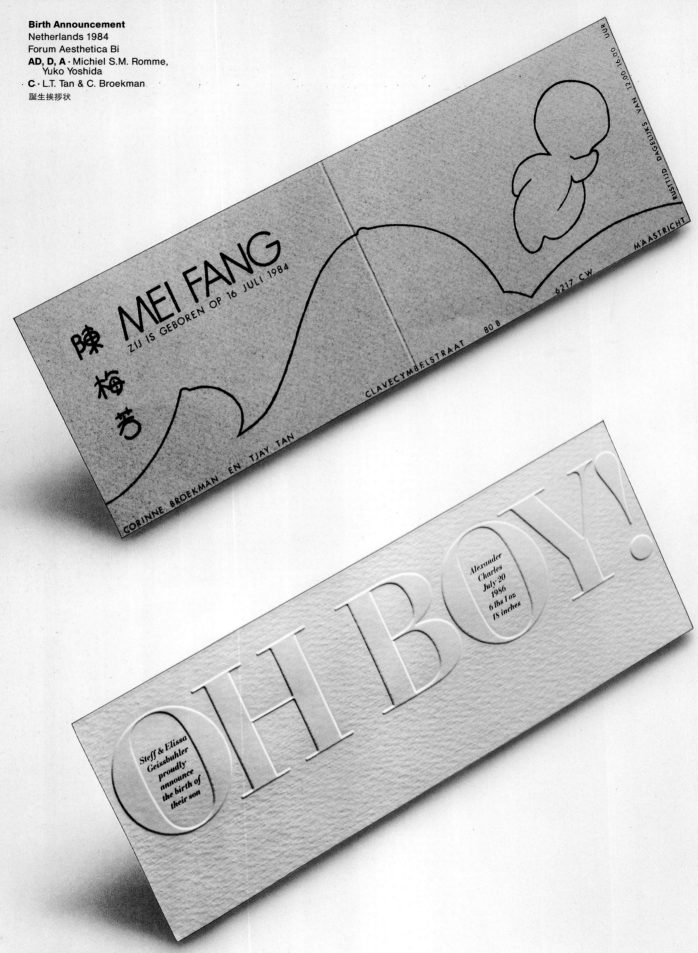

106

Birth Announcement
Netherlands 1984
Forum Aesthetica Bi
AD, D, A · Michiel S.M. Romme,
Yuko Yoshida
C · L.T. Tan & C. Broekman
誕生挨拶状

Birth Announcement
Graphic designer
USA 1986
Steff Geissbuhler
AD, D, A · Steff Geissbuhler
C · Steff Geissbuhler
誕生挨拶状

Season's Greetings Card
USA 1987/88
Laughlin/Winkler
AD, D · Mark Laughlin,
Ellen Winkler
C · Notter Finegold + Alexander
Inc.
季節の挨拶状

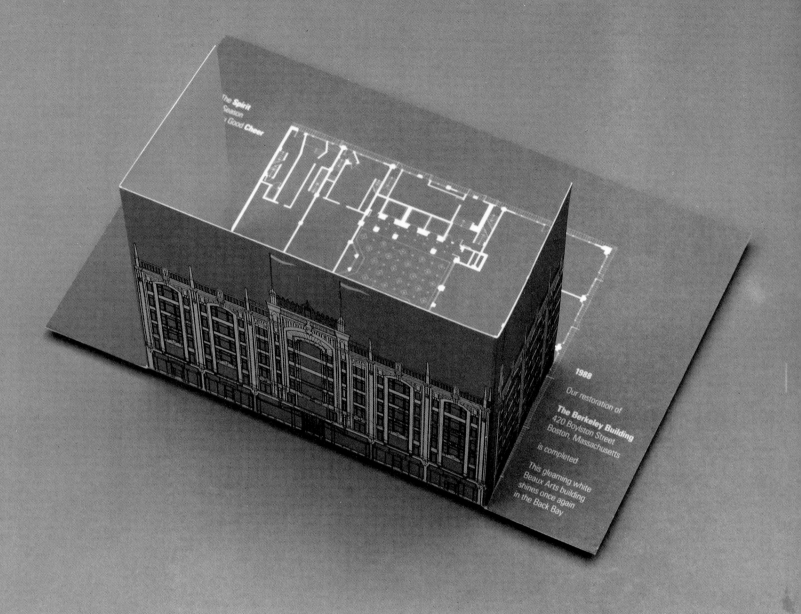

Season's Greetings Card
Graphic design firm
India 1976
Desilva Associates
AD, D, A · Roby J.F. D'Silva
C · Desilva Associates
季節の挨拶状
グラフィックデザイン会社

Invitation Card
Galleries and shops
Switzerland 1970–80
BBV
AD, D · Michael Baviera
C · Various clients
招待状
ギャラリー/ショップ

New Year's Card
Argentina 1982
Estudio Hache
AD, D · Alfredo Halmayer,
 Marcelo Varela
C · Bayer Argentina S.A.
年賀状

Party Invitation
Graphic design firm
Australia 1986
Emery Vincent Associates
AD, D, A · Emery Vincent
Associates
C · Inarc Design Pty. Ltd.
パーティ招待状

INARC: NOW WE ARE FIFTEEN

We invite you to share an evening with us at H's South Yarra on Tuesday 17 June 1986 at 6.00pm.

In our fifteenth year we thought this a good time to reacquaint you with Inarc, discuss new directions for 1986

Christmas Card
The Cuban Pavilion, Osaka
México 1969
Félix Beltrán & Associates
AD, D, A · Félix Beltrán
C · Félix Beltrán,
Attn. Pabellon Cubano
クリスマスカード
大阪万博キューバ館

Season's Greetings Card
Engineering company
Argentina 1978
Gustavo Pedroza, Comunicación
Visual
AD, D, A · Gustavo Pedroza
C · Techint S.A.
季節の挨拶状
エンジニアリング会社

Party Invitation
USA 1986
ABC Television Network
AD · Bill Duevell, Christina
 Sanchez
D · Christina Sanchez, William
 Olivari
A · Fred Dreany
C · ABC/Sports
パーティ招待状

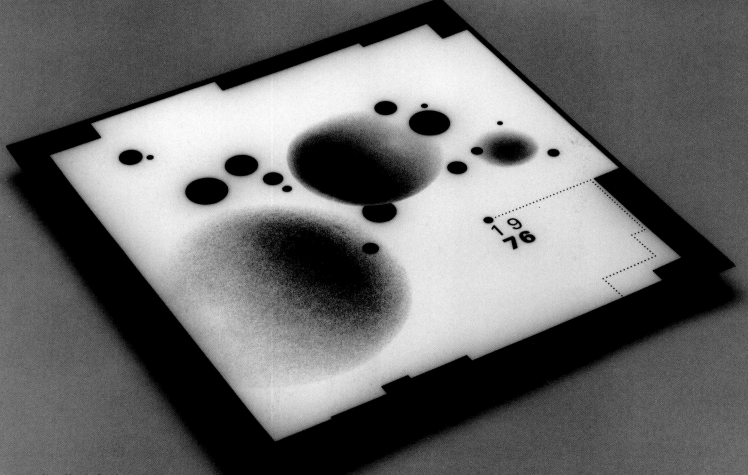

New Year's Card
Graphic designer
USA 1975
Gregory Thomas Associates
AD, D, A · Gregory Thomas
C · Gregory Thomas
年賀状
グラフィックデザイナー

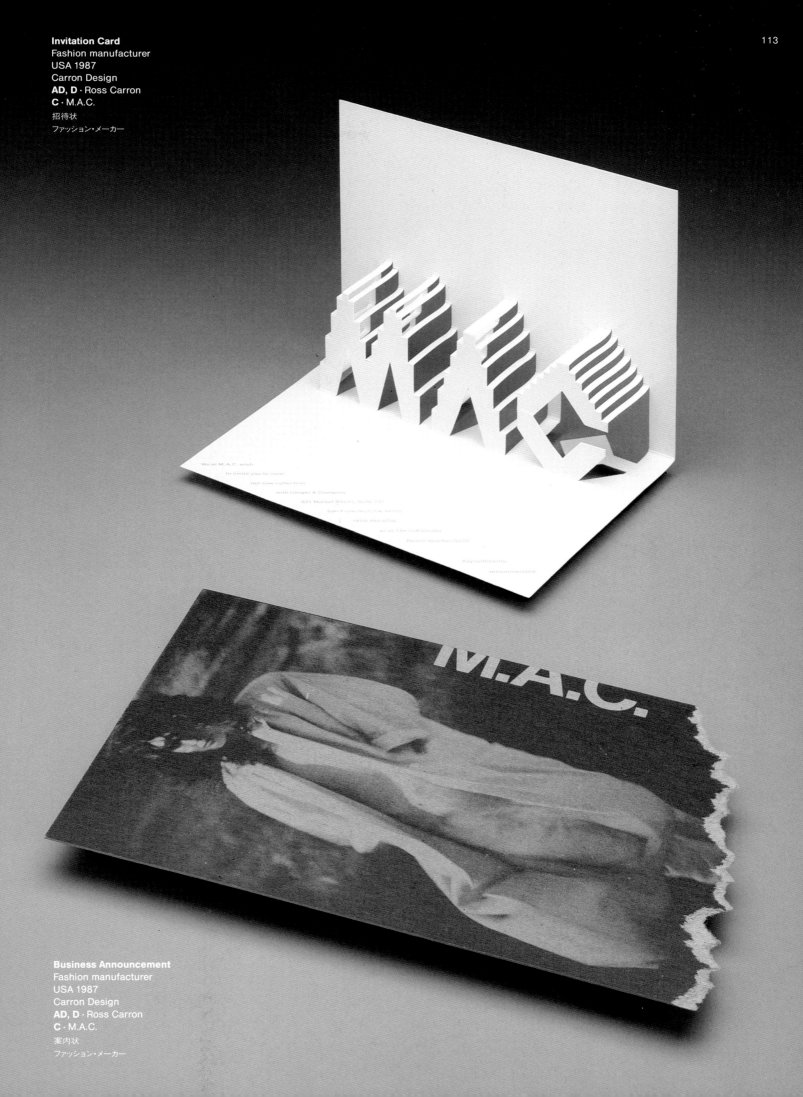

Invitation Card
Fashion manufacturer
USA 1987
Carron Design
AD, D · Ross Carron
C · M.A.C.
招待状
ファッション・メーカー

Business Announcement
Fashion manufacturer
USA 1987
Carron Design
AD, D · Ross Carron
C · M.A.C.
案内状
ファッション・メーカー

Christmas Card
Architectural society
Canada 1972
Rolf Harder & Associates Inc.
AD, D, A · Rolf Harder
C · Ordre des Architectes du
　　Québec

クリスマスカード
建築協会

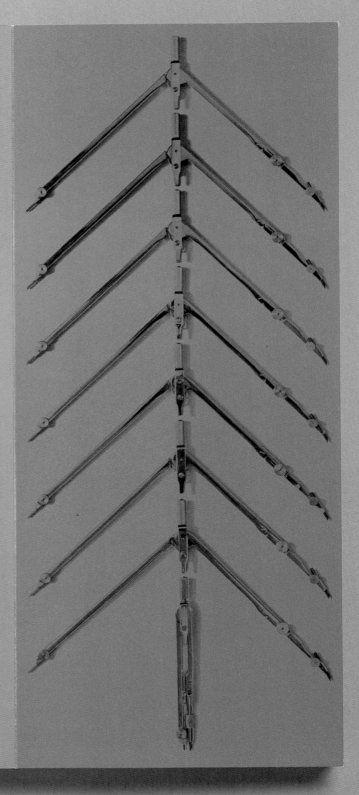

The President and Council
of the Province of Quebec
Association of Architects
send greetings and best wishes
for Christmas and the New Year

Le Président et le Conseil
de l'Association des Architectes
de la Province de Québec
vous offrent leurs meilleurs voeux à
l'occasion de Noël et du Nouvel An

Christmas Card
Museum
USA 1985
Igarashi Studio
AD · Takenobu Igarashi
D · Aya Usami
C · The Museum of Modern Art,
New York

クリスマスカード
美術館
(「Ho Ho」は，トナカイの鳴き声)

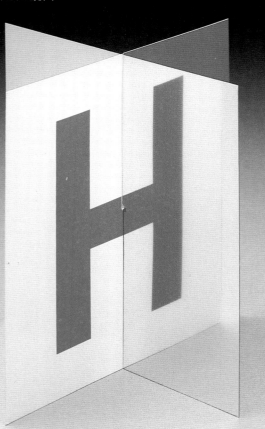

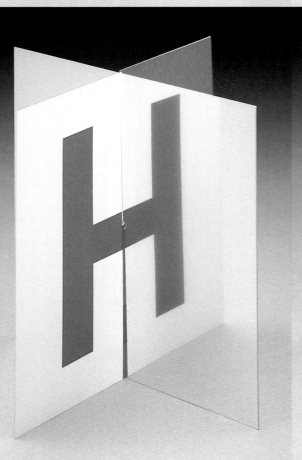
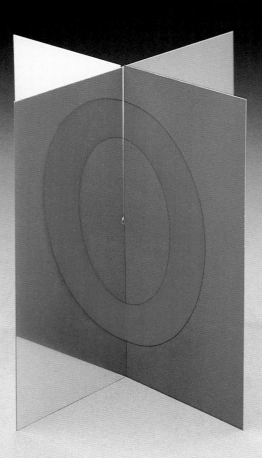

116

ON BEHALF OF THE GATEWAY
HOMART DEVELOPMENT CO.
THE "OFFICIAL REAL ESTATE DEVELOPER"
AND A SPONSOR OF THE
1988 VIRGINIA SLIMS OF CALIFORNIA
TENNIS TOURNAMENT
INVITES YOU TO A PRE-MATCH PARTY
ON "HOMART NIGHT"
THURSDAY, FEBRUARY 18   5:30 – 7:00 PM
OAKLAND COLISEUM ARENA
PACIFIC ROOM, LOWER LEVEL
695 HEGENBERGER ROAD
OAKLAND, CALIFORNIA

COCKTAILS
HORS D'OEUVRES
GIFTS

RSVP BY
MONDAY, FEBRUARY 15
415.583.3850

TENNIS MATCH BEGINS 7:00 PM

You are cordially invited to attend the
Fifth Annual Waldenbooks Marketing Presentation
"A Look Back At '85 And A Look Ahead To '86"
Featuring hors d'oeuvres and dessert by Martha Stewart.

Thursday, February 20, 1986. Astor Hall, The New York Public Library
42nd Street at 5th Avenue. 6:30 p.m. Cocktails and Hors D'Oeuvres
7:30 p.m. Presentation 8:30 p.m. Dessert and Champagne
RSVP by Feb. 14 (203) 356-7505/7710 Please enter thru 42nd St. entrance

Expansion Announcement
Dentists
USA 1988
The Design Office of Wong & Yeo
AD, D, A · Valerie Wong
C · Yoshikawa, DDS / Lee, DDS
事業拡張案内状
歯科医師

Christmas Card
Graphic design firm
USA 1987
Design Forum
AD · Bill Chidley
D · Renae Roberts
C · Design Forum
クリスマスカード
グラフィックデザイン会社

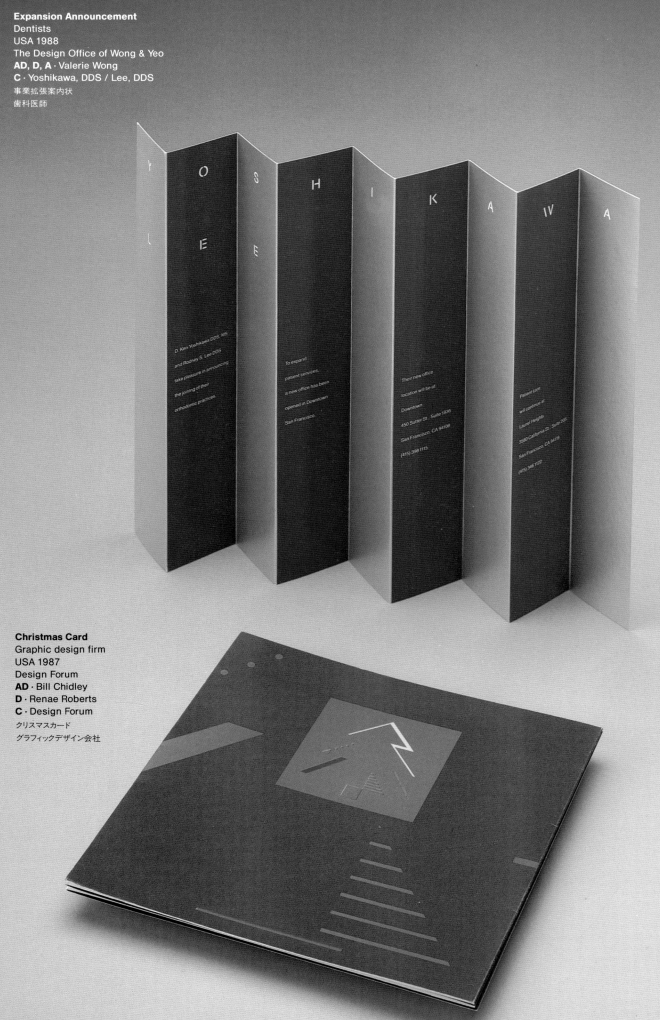

Season's Greetings Card
Graphic design firm
USA 1984
H.L.Chu & Co., Ltd.
AD, D, A · Hoi L. Chu
C · H.L.Chu & Co., Ltd.
季節の挨拶状
グラフィックデザイン会社

Moving Announcement
Netherlands 1987
Samenwerkende Ontwerpers
AD, D · André Toet
A · André Thijssen
C · KVGO-FGE
移転通知状

New Year's Card
Netherlands 1986
Samenwerkende Ontwerpers
AD, D · André Toet
A · Maarten van de Velde
C · FGE, Alwin van Steijn
年賀状

Moving Announcement
Graphic designer
USA 1988
Vanderbeek & Chiow Advertising
AD, D, A · David Chiow
C · David Chiow
移転通知状
グラフィックデザイナー

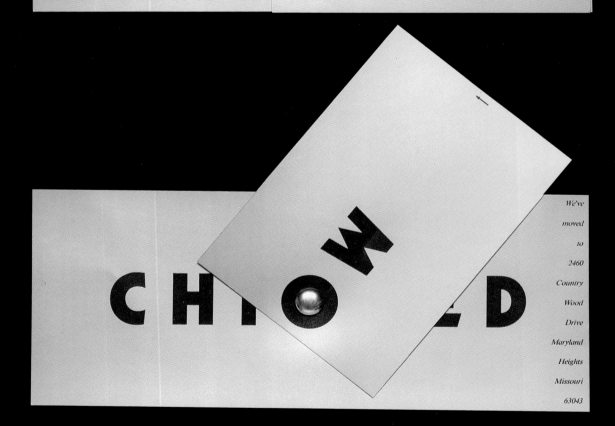

Season's Greetings Card
Graphic design firm
USA 1971
Bass/Yager & Associates
AD, D · Saul Bass
A · Saul Bass, Art Goodman
C · Bass/Yager & Associates
季節の挨拶状
グラフィックデザイン会社

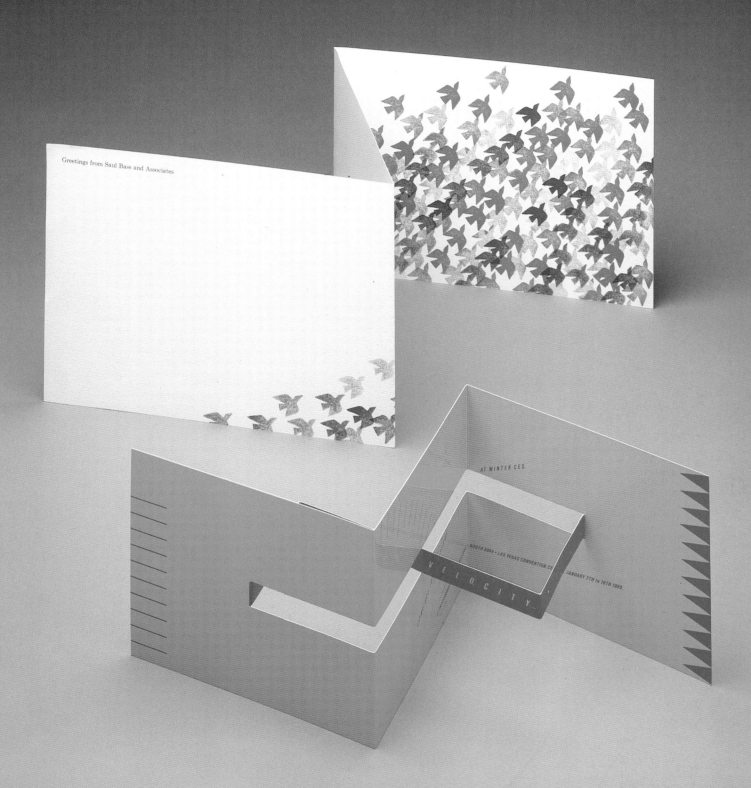

Trade Show Invitation
USA 1988
The Design Office of Wong & Yeo
AD, D, A · Hock Wah Yeo
C · Velocity
商品見本市招待状

Christmas Card
Model makers
England 1984
The Partners (Design Consultants) Ltd.
AD, D · David Stuart
C · Stephen Greenfield
(Take a moment to think about this one)
クリスマスカード
模型メーカー
（３つの四角形のな
かをこすると，におい
がするはずですが…）

A *scratch* ® *'n sniff* CHRISTMAS CARD

VODKA

TURKEY (DEEP FROZEN)

SNOW

Wedding Invitation
Hong Kong 1984
Kan Tai-keung Design & Associates Ltd.
AD, D · Freeman Lau
C · Bernald and Jacqueline
結婚式招待状

Bernard & Jacqueline

Commemorative
Announcement
USA 1988
Laughlin/Winkler
AD, D · Mark Laughlin, Ellen
   Winkler
C · Shepley Bulfinch Richardson
   and Abbott
周年記念挨拶状

H.H. Richardson proposed the design
of his seal in this letter to his
wife in 1882.

124 **Exhibition Announcement**
Graphic designer
Japan 1986
Time Space Art Inc.
AD · Hiroshi Morishima
D · Hiroshi Morishima, Katsumi
Komagata
C · Time Space Art Inc.
展覧会案内状
グラフィックデザイナー

TIE—*musubu*
To join strings
or ropes
together.
Also,
to become
betrothed or
reach maturity
and fruition.

EMPTINESS—*ku*
The sky,
void, or
the state
of limbo.
In Buddhism
all things
are regarded
as being
contained
within "*ku*".

FOLD—*oru*
To bind
or fold: used
especially
of paper
or cloth.

BEAUTY—*utsukushii*
Beauty or
appeal, and
by extension
that which
evokes
feelings of
pathos.

AN INVITATION TO THE **NIHONGA**

MOVE—*ugoku*
To change
positions or move
receptively.
The combination
of this
character
with the character
for "life" forms
a concept
used to
describe
the essence of
agitated motion
in some paintings,
stone drawings
or works of
calligraphy.

126

Christmas Card
Architectural society
Canada 1971
Rolf Harder & Associates Inc.
AD, D · Rolf Harder
C · Ordre des Architectes
du Québec
クリスマスカード
建築協会

New Year's Card
Graphic designer
Norway 1980/81
Enzo Finger
AD, D · Enzo Finger
C · Enzo Finger
年賀状
グラフィックデザイナー

Christmas Card
Concert organizing company
Hong Kong 1987
Alan Chan Design Co.
AD, D · Alan Chan
C · Artist World Enterprises Ltd.
クリスマスカード
コンサート企画会社

128　**Season's Greetings Card**
Illustrator
USA 1988
Robin Ghelerter
AD, D, A · Robin Ghelerter
C · Robin Ghelerter
季節の挨拶状
イラストレーター

Exhibition Announcement
Netherlands 1988
Samenwerkende Ontwerpers
AD, D · André Toet
C · KVGO
展覧会案内状

New Year's Card
Graphic design firm
Japan 1987
Ken Miki & Associates
AD, D · Ken Miki
C · Ken Miki & Associates
年賀状
グラフィックデザイン会社

A HAPPY NEW YEAR

New Year's Card
Japan 1986
Koji Tashiro
AD, D · Koji Tashiro
C · Koji Tashiro
年賀状

130

New Year's Card
USA
Lipson Alport Glass &
Associates
AD, D · Stan Brod
C · Stan Brod
年賀状

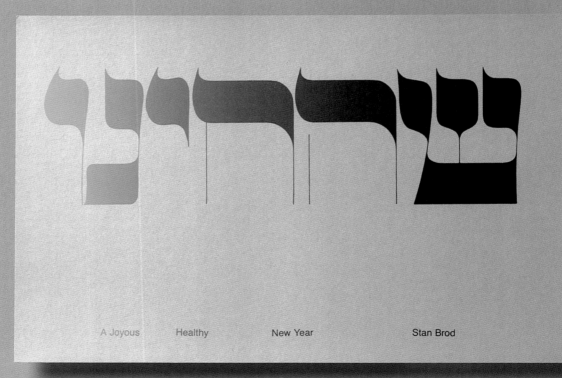

New Year's Card
USA
Lipson Alport Glass &
Associates
AD, D · Stan Brod
C · Stan Brod, McCrystle Wood
年賀状

Christmas Card
Graphic design firm
USA 1988
Zender + Associates, Inc.
AD, D, A · Nancy McIntosh
C · Zender + Associates, Inc.
クリスマスカード
グラフィックデザイン会社

...reat joy.

...vid, has been born for you a Savior,
...t the Lord.

May your hearts be full of love & joy.   Zender + Associates, Inc.

Wir freuen uns
die Geburt
unserer Tochter Randy
bekanntzugeben.

geboren am 7. 7. 88
um 9.15 Uhr
3840 g schwer
55 cm groß

Francine Katikali
Udo Schliemann
Gaußstraße 107
7000 Stuttgart 1

y

Season's Greetings

Henry Steiner | Graphic Communication Ltd. Hong Kong

New Year's Card
Graphic designer
Hong Kong 1969
Graphic Communication Ltd.
AD, D · Henry Steiner
C · Graphic Communication Ltd.
(Cover reads "HAPPY NEW...")
年賀状
（表紙には"HAPPY NEW…"とある）

Christmas Card
Design consultants
Japan 1985
Igarashi Studio
AD · Takenobu Igarashi
D · Yukimi Sasago
C · Axis Ltd.
クリスマスカード
デザイン・コンサルティング会社

Moving Announcement
Graphic design firm
USA 1980
Crosby Associates Inc.
AD, D · Bart Crosby
C · Crosby Associates Inc.
移転通知状
グラフィックデザイン会社

◀ As of October 1, 1980 Bonnell and Crosby Inc. will be located in new offices at 676 St. Clair, Chicago 60611. Our new telephone number will be 312.951.2800.

134

Summer's Greetings Card
Graphic design firm
USA 1987
Weisz Yang Dunkelberger Inc.
AD · Larry Yang
D · Bernard Reynoso, Tracy Miller
C · Weisz Yang Dunkelberger
   Inc.
(Printed on actual sand paper)
夏の挨拶状
グラフィックデザイン会社
（サンド・ペーパーの上に印刷されている）

Summer's Greetings Card
Graphic design firm
USA 1988
Weisz Yang Dunkelberger Inc.
AD · Larry Yang
D · Mary Jane Broadbent, Tracy
   Miller
C · Weisz Yang Dunkelberger
   Inc.
(Plastic ants included)
夏の挨拶状
グラフィックデザイン会社
（プラスチック製のアリが入っている）

Christmas Card
Graphic design firm
USA 1987
Axion Design, Inc.
AD · Michele Garns
D · Sharon Till
C · Axion Design, Inc.
クリスマスカード
グラフィックデザイン会社

136

Wedding Invitation
Hong Kong 1988
Kan Tai-keung Design &
Associates Ltd.
AD · Kan Tai-keung
D · C. Ng
C · Joanna and Robert
結婚式招待状

Moving Announcement
Australia 1987
Cozzolino/Ellett Design D'Vison
AD · Mimmo Cozzolino
D · Rosanna Dirisio
A · Louis Cagalj
C · Tomasetti Copy Paper
移転通知状

TOMASETTI COPY PAPER A

THANKS TO THE ENTHUSIASTIC SUPPORT YOU'VE GIVEN US OVER THE PAST FEW YEARS, WE'VE OUTGROWN OUR PRESENT WAREHO

MOVING!

D BIGGER PREMISES. SO, FROM 10 AUGUST 1987 YOU'LL FIND US AT 29 LIONEL ROAD MT. WAVERLEY 3149. PHONE (03) 544 2777, FAX (03) 544 7258.

K

The world awaits Kris **K**ringle, Father Christmas and St. Nicholas, too.

L

Fa, La, La, La, La, La, La, La, La

Season's Greetings Booklet
Graphic design firm
USA 1984
Pat Hansen Design
AD · Pat Hansen
D, A · Pat Hansen, Paula
  Richards
C · Pat Hansen Design
季節の挨拶状（小冊子）
グラフィックデザイン会社

Expansion Announcement
Interior design firm
USA 1986
Pat Hansen Design
AD · Pat Hansen
D · Jesse Doquilo, Pat Hansen
C · FORMA
事業拡張挨拶状
インテリアデザイン会社

事業拡張挨拶状
インテリアデザイン会社

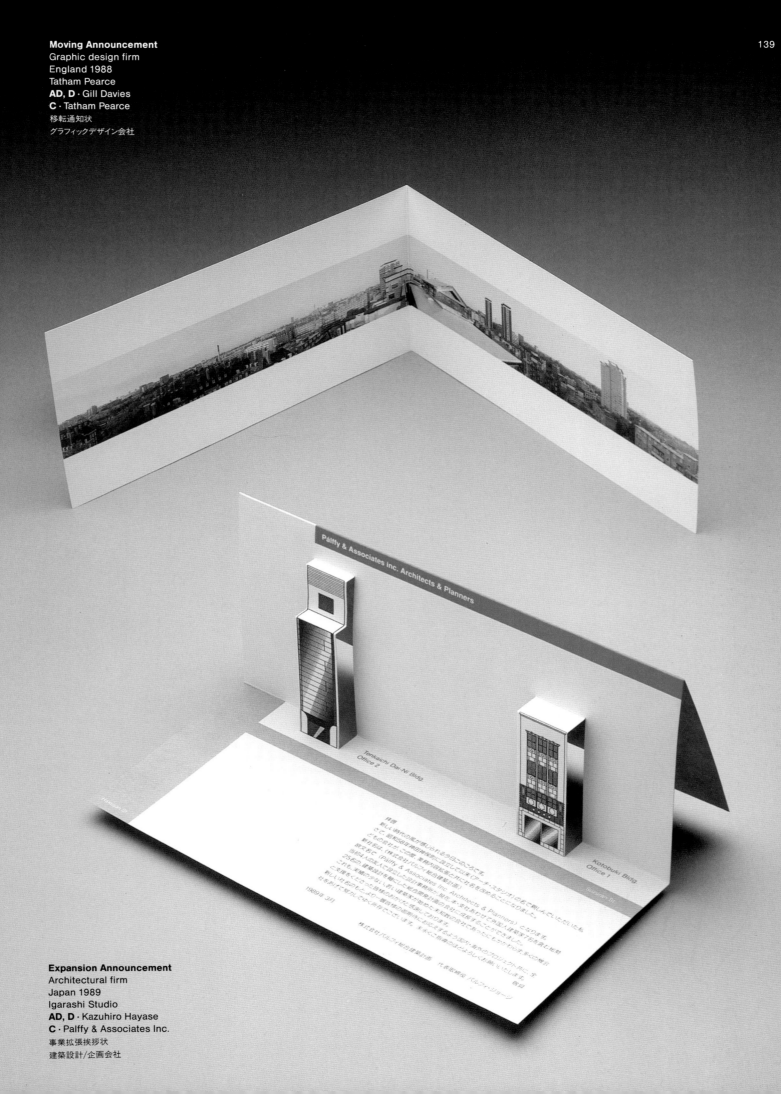

Moving Announcement
Graphic design firm
England 1988
Tatham Pearce
AD, D · Gill Davies
C · Tatham Pearce
移転通知状
グラフィックデザイン会社

Expansion Announcement
Architectural firm
Japan 1989
Igarashi Studio
AD, D · Kazuhiro Hayase
C · Palffy & Associates Inc.
事業拡張挨拶状
建築設計/企画会社

**Environmental Exhibition
Invitation**
Netherlands 1987
Samenwerkende Ontwerpers
AD, D · Marianne Vos
C · Museon
環境展招待状

Symposium Invitation
Netherlands 1988
Samenwerkende Ontwerpers
AD, D · André Toet
A · Maarten van de Velde
C · Culturele Raad Zuid-Holland
シンポジューム招待状

Party Invitation
England 1984
Trickett & Webb Ltd.
AD · Lynn Trickett, Brian Webb
D · Simon Blowning, Lynn
   Trickett, Brian Webb
A · Chris Brown
C · Augustus Martin
パーティ招待状

Season's Greetings Card
Building company
Netherlands 1986
Total Design bv
AD, D · Frans Lieshout
C · Macobouw bv
季節の挨拶状
建築会社

Nightclub Opening Invitation
Australia 1986
Flett Henderson & Arnold
AD · Richard Henderson
D, A · Flett Henderson & Arnold
C · Hyatt On Collins
ナイトクラブ・オープニング招待状

Christmas Card
USA 1987
Paul Davis Studio
AD, A · Paul Davis
D · Jose Conde
C · Manhattan Plaza
クリスマスカード

144

Expansion Announcement
Graphic design firm
USA 1981
Louis Nelson Associates Inc.
AD, D · Louis Nelson
C · Louis Nelson Associates Inc.
事業拡張挨拶状
グラフィックデザイン会社

Louis Nelson
Associates Inc

Designers
and
Planners

80
University Place
New York
10003

212 620 9191

and
we're growing!

in a
beautiful, new,
sunny space,

with
talented people.

I have
a new office,

Moving Announcement
Graphic designer
Netherlands 1983
Samenwerkende Ontwerpers
AD, D · André Toet
C · Marianne Vos
移転通知状
グラフィックデザイナー

Christmas Card
USA 1988
F. Ron Miller
AD, D, A · F. Ron Miller
C · F. Ron Miller
(Photograph with corrugated
cardboard frame)
クリスマスカード
（ダンボールのフレームに写真ををはめてあ
る）

Christmas Cards
Designer's family
England 1957
W M de Majo Associates
AD, D · W M de Majo MBE FCSD,
  Veronica de Majo
C · W M de Majo Associates
クリスマスカード
デザイナーの家族

Postcards
Australia 1981
Cozzolino Hughes
AD · Mimmo Cozzolino
D · David Hughes, Mimmo
Cozzolino
A · David Hughes
C · Cozzolino Hughes
ポストカード

148

Christmas Card
Magazine
USA 1983
Milton Glaser, Inc.
AD · Alexander Lieberman
D, A · Milton Glaser
C · Vanity Fair
クリスマスカード
雑誌

Cheers!

SEASON'S GREETINGS

WOW!

...8, 1988
...6 10:00 pm
23822 Mercury Road
El Toro
California

RSVP
by December 9th
Barbara
714/660-0970
CYP, Inc.
Architecture/Planning

Season's Greetings Card
Architectural firm
USA 1988
The Victor Group, Inc.
AD · Noel Davies
D · Meredith Kamm
C · CYP, Inc.
季節の挨拶状
建築設計会社

Christmas Card
Graphic design firm
USA 1978
Witherspoon Design
AD, D, A · Randy Lynn
Witherspoon
C · Witherspoon Design

クリスマスカード
グラフィックデザイン会社

Postcards
England 1987
Pentagram Design Ltd.
AD · David Hillman
D · David Hillman, Amanda
Bennett
C · OUN International
(3 from a set of 200
"Puzzlegram" postcards —
answers on back)
ポストカード
（200枚のポスト・カードがそれぞれ異なった
パズルで，裏に答が書かれている）

Place a coin on any point of the star and slide it along to another point. Place a second coin on any vacant point and similarly slide it along a line to reach another open point. Continue in the same manner until seven coins have been placed on seven points, leaving only one vacant.

How would you cut a hole in one cube to enable another identically-sized cube to pass through it?

Two cyclists do laps across circular paths each one-third of a mile long. They start simultaneously at the black spots with speeds of six miles and thirteen miles per hour. By the end of the act, how many times will they have simultaneously returned to the spots where they started?

Product Announcement
USA 1988
Willi Kunz Associates Inc.
AD, D, A · Willi Kunz
C · The Steelcase Design
　　Partnership
製品紹介の挨拶状

The Steelcase Design Partnership cordially invites you to an exclusive Chicago area post-Neocon presentation of its new product introductions.

Thursday, July 21, 1988

5.00–8.00pm

The Steelcase Design Partnership Companies'
Merchandise Mart Showrooms, Chicago

Atelier International
Space 9-100
Brayton International
Space 1168
Metropolitan Furniture
Space 11-100
Vecta Contract
Space 305

erry Christmas

Christmas Card
England 1987
The Partners (Design
Consultants) Ltd.
AD · David Stuart
D · Martin Devlin
C · Data Logic
クリスマスカード

152

New Year's Card
Graphic design firm
Netherlands 1986
Total Design bv
AD, D · Frans Lieshout
C · Total Design bv
年賀状
グラフィックデザイン会社

Moving Announcement
Graphic design firm
Netherlands 1987
Total Design bv
AD, D · Frans Lieshout
C · Total Design bv
移転通知状
グラフィックデザイン会社

Wedding Invitation
USA 1987
The Appelbaum Company
AD, D · Harvey Appelbaum
C · Harvey Appelbaum
結婚式招待状

Birth Announcement
USA 1988
Hannah Smotrich
AD, D · Hannah Smotrich
C · Maura and Mark Shapiro
誕生挨拶状

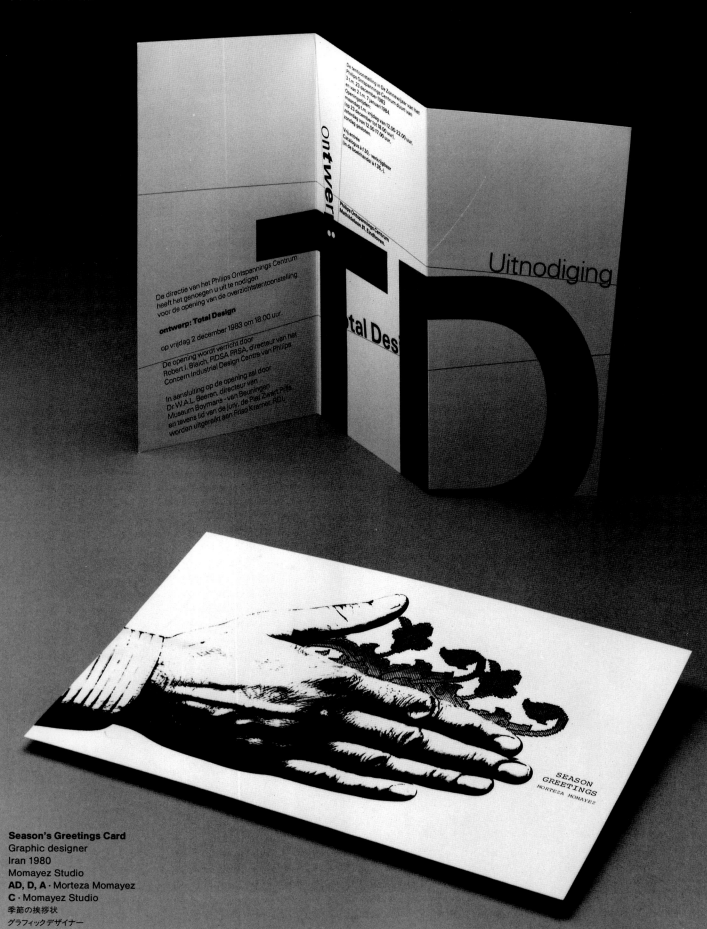

154 **Invitation Card**
Graphic design firm
Netherlands 1983
Total Design bv
AD, D · Frans Lieshout
C · Total Design bv
招待状
グラフィックデザイン会社

Season's Greetings Card
Graphic designer
Iran 1980
Momayez Studio
AD, D, A · Morteza Momayez
C · Momayez Studio
季節の挨拶状
グラフィックデザイナー

ARGENTINA

Daniel Higa Diseño y Comunicación Visual
French 2279
Buenos Aires 1125
Argentina
17

Estudio Hache S.A.
Arcos 2680
Buenos Aires 1428
Argentina
109

Gustavo Pedroza Comunicación Visual
Carlos Calvo 482, 2° piso.
Buenos Aires 1102
Argentina
111

Shakespear/Estudio de Diseño
Juan José Diaz 594
San Isidro
Buenos Aires 1642
Argentina
86

AUSTRALIA

Annette Harcus Design
30-36 Bay Street, Double Bay
Sydney, NSW 2028
Australia
21, 22

Barrie Tucker Design Pty. Ltd.
4/245 Fullarton Road
Eastwood, SA 5063
Australia
78

Con Aslanis
1/40 Green Street
Prahran, Victoria 3181
Australia
104

Cozzolino/Ellett Design D'Vision
P.O. Box 198
Heidelberg, Victoria 3084
Australia
136, 147

Emery Vincent Associates
80 Market Street
South Melbourne, Victoria 3205
Australia
110

Flett Henderson & Arnold
Unit 1/663 Victoria Street
Abbotsford, Victoria 3067
Australia
49, 84, 143

CANADA

Eskind Weddell
260 Richmond ST. West 201
Toronto, Ontario M5V 1W5
Canada
32, 100

Furman Graphic Design
400 Slater Street
Suite 1507
Ottawa, Ontario K1R 7S7
Canada
88

Kramer Design Associates Ltd.
103 Dupont Street
Toronto, Ontario M5R 1V4
Canada
42

Rolf Harder & Assoc., Inc.
1350 Sherbrooke St. W., 1000
Montreal, Quebec H3G 1J1
Canada
114, 126

Rushton, Green and Grossutti Inc.
905 Broadview Avenue
Toronto, Ontario M4K 2R2
Canada
49, 64

ENGLAND

CarterWong Ltd.
7 Royalty Studios
105 Lancaster Road
London W11 1QF
England
9

Julia Alldridge Associates
7 Primrose Mews
1A Sharpleshall Street
London NW1 8YW
England
61

KB Design
18 Pindock Mews
London W9 2PY
England
14

Liz James Design Associates
18 Pindock Mews
London W9 2PY
England
93

Minale, Tattersfield and Partners Ltd.
The Courtyard, 37 Sheen Road
Richmond, Surry TW91AJ
England
68, 84, 98

Pentagram Design Ltd.
11 Needham Road
London W11 2RP
England
46, 53, 88, 150

Tatham Pearce Ltd.
9 Hatton Street
London NW8 8PL
England
139

NETHERLANDS

Forum Aesthetica Bi
Capucijnenstraat 69
6211 RP Maastricht
Netherlands
106

Frans Lieshout
Geesterduingweg 184
1902 CC Castricum
Netherlands
48

Maarten Vijgenboom Design
Houtstraat 15
5911 JB Venlo
Netherlands
71

Samenwerkende Ontwerpers
Herengracht 160
1016 BN Amsterdam
Netherlands
57, 119, 128, 140, 141, 144

Total Design bv
Van Diemenstraat 200
1013 CP Amsterdam
Netherlands
74, 142, 152, 154

NORWAY

Enzo Finger Design
Skogryggreien 7B
0389 Oslo 3
Norway
50, 52, 126

SPAIN

Estudio Pla-Narbona
Carrer Nou, 12 - 08394
Sant Vicenc de Montalt
Spain
55, 80

SWITZERLAND

BBV
Zeltweg 7
Zürich, CH-8032
Switzerland
59, 86, 108

Gottschalk + Ash International
Sonnhaldenstrasse 3
8030 Zürich
Switzerland
30, 56, 92

Louis Mermet Grafic ASG
Stiftsgasse 5
CH-4051 Basel
Switzerland
48

USA

Axion Design, Inc.
P.O. Box 629
San Anselmo, CA 94960
USA
135

Carron Design
340 Lombard Street
San Francisco CA 94133
USA
51, 113

Chermayeff & Geismar Associates
15 East 26th Street
New York, NY 10010
USA
21

Christina Sanchez
ABC Television Network
Capital Cities/ABC
77 West 66th Street
New York, NY 10023
USA
112

Concrete
633 South Plymouth Court
Suite 208
Chicago, IL 60605
USA
28, 116

Crosby Associates Inc.
676 N. St. Clair
Suit 1805
Chicago, IL 60611
USA
10, 11, 66, 67, 80, 133

Cross Associates
10513 W. Pico Boulevard
Los Angeles, CA 90064
USA
29

David Leigh
1245 Park Avenue
New york, NY 10128
USA
28, 70

de Harak & Poulin Associates, Inc.
320 West 13th Street
New York, NY 10014
USA
37

Design Forum
2322 Far Hills Avenue
Dayton, OH 45419
USA
117

F. Ron Miller
10937 1/2 Camarillo
North Hollywood, CA 91602
USA
145

Federico Design
Route 3 Box 242
Pound Ridge, NY 10576
USA
34, 35

Follis Design
2124 Venice Boulevard
Los Angeles, CA 90006-5299
USA
16

G. Salchow Design
843 Clifton Hills Terrace
Cincinnati, OH 45220
USA
73

Gina Federico Graphic Design
71 Park Place
New Canaan, CT 06840
USA
24, 94

Gregory Thomas Associates
2238 1/2 Purdue Avenue
Los Angeles, CA 90064
USA
112

H.L. Chu & Company, Ltd.
39 West 29th Street
New York, NY 10001
USA
63, 96, 118

Hannah Smotrich
244 West 72nd / Apt.3C
New York, NY 10023
USA
153

LaPine/O'Very
701 East South Temple
Salt Lake City, UT 84102
USA
9, 12, 39

Laughlin/Winkler
205 A Street
Boston, MA 02210
USA
81, 107, 123

Lipson Alport Glass & Associates
2349 Victory Parkway
Cincinnati, OH 45206
USA
26, 52, 54, 130

Louis Nelson Associates Inc.
80 University Place
New York, NY 10003
USA
25, 144

Luci Goodman Studio
6209 17th Avenue NE
Seattle, WA 98115
USA
18, 65

M Plus M, Inc.
17 Cornelia Street
New York, NY 10014
USA
13

Mark Anderson Design
2133 Stockton Street, Apt.A303
San Francisco, CA 94133
USA
62

Mike Quon Office, Inc.
568 Broadway Suite 703
New York, NY 10012
USA
94, 105

Milton Glaser, Inc.
207 East 32nd Street
New York, NY 10016
USA
148

Murrie-White, Drummond, Lienhart & Associates
58 West Hurron
Chicago, IL 60610
USA
55

Pat Hansen Design
618 Second Avenue, Suite 1080
Seattle, WA 98104
USA
22, 45, 137, 138

Paul Davis Studio
14 East 4th Street, 504
New York, NY 10012
USA
143

Peter Walberg Design
825 Superba Avenue
Venice, CA 90291
USA
98

Richardson Smith Inc.
139 Lewis Wharf
Boston, MA 02110
USA
47

Robin Ghelerter
1118 S. Sherbourne Drive #1
Los Angeles, CA 90035
USA
128

Ross McBride
1123 Perry HWY
Pittsburgh, PA 15237
USA
43

Saul Bass/Herb Yager & Associates
7039 Sunset Boulevard
Los Angeles, CA 90028
USA
121

Shimokochi/Reeves Design
6043 Hollywood Boulevard
Suite 203
Los Angeles, CA 90028
USA
79

Skolos Wedell + Raynor, Inc.
The Schrafft Center
529 Main Street
Charlestown, MA 02129
USA
85

Steff Geissbuhler
60 Hollywood Drive,
Hastings-on-Hudson
New York, NY 10706
USA
106

Sussman/Prejza + Company, Inc.
1651 18th Street
Santa Monica, CA 90404
USA
90

Tandem Studios
324 South 400 West
Salt Lake City, UT 84101
USA
75

The Appelbaum Company
176 Madison Avenue
New York, NY 10016
USA
153

The Design Office of Wong & Yeo
744 Union Street #1
San Francisco, CA 94133
USA
31, 44, 63, 117, 121

The Victor Group, Inc.
5817 Uplander Way
Culver City, CA 90230
USA
148

**The Weller Institute
for the Cure of Design, Inc.**
P.O. Box 726, 1398 Aerie Drive
Park City, UT 84060
USA
16

UCI, Inc.
1088 Bishop Street, Suite 1226
Honolulu, HI 96813
USA
14, 44

Vanderbeek & Chiow Advertising
130 S. Bemiston Avenue
St. Louis, MO 63105
USA
120

Vita/Design
120 Belgrave Avenue
San Francisco, CA 94117
USA
38

Weisz Yang Dunkelberger Inc.
61 Wilton Road
Westport, CT 06880
USA
51, 116, 134

White + Associates
137 North Virgil Avenue #204
Los Angeles, CA 90004
USA
46

Willy Kunz Associates Inc.
2112 Broadway
New York, NY 10023
USA
95, 97, 151

Witherspoon Design
1844 West 5th Avenue
Columbus, OH 43212
USA
149

Zender + Associates, Inc.
2311 Park Avenue
Cincinnati, OH 45206
USA
29, 36, 101, 131

WEST GERMANY

Mendell & Oberer
Widenmayerstr. 12
8000 München 22
West Germany
82

Teunen & Teunen
Post Fach 36
6222 Geisenheim 2
West Germany
68

Udo Schliemann
Gausstrasse 107
Stuttgart-1 7000
West Germany
132

WEST INDIES

Russel Halfhide Graphic Design
28 Angelina Street
St. James
Port of Spain, Trinidad
West Indies
89

GREETING CARDS
世界のグリーティング・カード

1989 年 9 月 25 日　　初版第 1 刷発行
1990 年 6 月 25 日　　初版第 2 刷発行

編者　　　　　　　　五十嵐威暢 ©
発行者　　　　　　　久世利郎
印刷所　　　　　　　凸版印刷株式会社
製本所　　　　　　　凸版印刷株式会社
発行所　　　　　　　株式会社グラフィック社
　　　　　　　　　　〒102　東京都千代田区九段北 1-9-12
　　　　　　　　　　電話 03(263)4318　振替・東京 3-114345
　　　　　　　　　　落丁・乱丁はお取替え致します。

監修　　　　　　　　　　五十嵐威暢
アートディレクション　　五十嵐威暢
カバー・デザイン　　　　ロス・ミクブライド
レイアウト　　　　　　　ロス・ミクブライド
撮影　　　　　　　　　　エド・イクタ
　　　　　　　　　　　　ナカサ＆パートナーズ
序文翻訳　　　　　　　　スコット・ブラウス
写真植字　　　　　　　　株式会社リンクス
　　　　　　　　　　　　三和写真工芸株式会社
グラフィック社編集担当　奥田政喜

ISBN4-7661-0537-0 C3070